THE BEDFORD SERIES IN HISTORY AND CULTURE

Napoleonic Foot Soldiers and Civilians

A Brief History with Documents

Related Titles in
THE BEDFORD SERIES IN HISTORY AND CULTURE
Advisory Editors: Lynn Hunt, *University of California, Los Angeles*
David W. Blight, *Yale University*
Bonnie G. Smith, *Rutgers University*
Natalie Zemon Davis, *Princeton University*
Ernest R. May, *Harvard University*

Louis XIV and Absolutism: A Brief Study with Documents
William Beik, *Emory University*

The Enlightenment: A Brief History with Documents
Margaret C. Jacob, *University of California, Los Angeles*

The French Revolution and Human Rights: A Brief Documentary History
Edited, Translated, and with an Introduction by Lynn Hunt, *University of California, Los Angeles*

DISCOURSE ON THE ORIGIN AND FOUNDATIONS OF INEQUALITY AMONG MEN *by Jean-Jacques Rousseau with Related Documents*
Translated, Edited, and with an Introduction by Helena Rosenblatt, *The Graduate Center of the City University of New York*

CANDIDE *by Voltaire*
Translated, Edited, and with an Introduction by Daniel Gordon, *University of Massachusetts Amherst*

Napoleon: Symbol for an Age: A Brief History with Documents
Rafe Blaufarb, *Florida State University*

Napoleonic Foot Soldiers and Civilians

A Brief History with Documents

Rafe Blaufarb

Florida State University

and

Claudia Liebeskind

Florida State University

BEDFORD / ST. MARTIN'S   Boston ◆ New York

For Bedford/St. Martin's

Publisher for History: Mary V. Dougherty
Director of Development for History: Jane Knetzger
Senior Editor: Heidi L. Hood
Developmental Editor: Debra Michals
Editorial Assistant: Jennifer Jovin
Production Associate: Samuel Jones
Executive Marketing Manager: Jenna Bookin Barry
Project Management: Books By Design, Inc.
Index: Books By Design, Inc.
Text Design: Claire Seng-Niemoeller
Cover Design: Andrea M. Corbin
Cover Art: © Museo Nacional del Prado–Madrid (Spain)
Composition: Achorn International
Printing and Binding: Haddon Craftsmen, Inc., an RR Donnelley & Sons Company

President: Joan E. Feinberg
Editorial Director: Denise B. Wydra
Editor in Chief: Karen S. Henry
Director of Marketing: Karen R. Soeltz
Director of Production: Susan W. Brown
Associate Director, Editorial Production: Elise S. Kaiser
Manager, Publishing Services: Andrea Cava

Library of Congress Control Number: 2010932691

Manufactured in the United States of America.

6   5   4   3   2   1
f   e   d   c   b   a

For information, write: Bedford/St. Martin's, 75 Arlington Street, Boston, MA 02116
(617-399-4000)

ISBN-13: 978-0-312-48700-3

Distributed outside North America by PALGRAVE MACMILLAN.

Foreword

The Bedford Series in History and Culture is designed so that readers can study the past as historians do.

The historian's first task is finding the evidence. Documents, letters, memoirs, interviews, pictures, movies, novels, or poems can provide facts and clues. Then the historian questions and compares the sources. There is more to do than in a courtroom, for hearsay evidence is welcome, and the historian is usually looking for answers beyond act and motive. Different views of an event may be as important as a single verdict. How a story is told may yield as much information as what it says.

Along the way the historian seeks help from other historians and perhaps from specialists in other disciplines. Finally, it is time to write, to decide on an interpretation and how to arrange the evidence for readers.

Each book in this series contains an important historical document or group of documents, each document a witness from the past and open to interpretation in different ways. The documents are combined with some element of historical narrative—an introduction or a biographical essay, for example—that provides students with an analysis of the primary source material and important background information about the world in which it was produced.

Each book in the series focuses on a specific topic within a specific historical period. Each provides a basis for lively thought and discussion about several aspects of the topic and the historian's role. Each is short enough (and inexpensive enough) to be a reasonable one-week assignment in a college course. Whether as classroom or personal reading, each book in the series provides firsthand experience of the challenge— and fun—of discovering, recreating, and interpreting the past.

Lynn Hunt
David W. Blight
Bonnie G. Smith
Natalie Zemon Davis
Ernest R. May

Preface

Few subjects in European history generate as much interest as the Napoleonic Wars. Fascination with them transcends national boundaries and has spawned thousands of histories. Most focus on campaigns and battles, narrating grand strategy, military operations, and tactics. These histories are complemented by contemporary memoirs, mainly by generals and officers. The generals tend to offer an Olympian overview of strategic movements, while the officers usually present highly embellished accounts of battlefield heroics. Whether military histories or memoirs, these works all treat the Napoleonic Wars from a narrowly military perspective. In them, combat dominates the storyline, and warriors are the main characters.

This volume strives for a broader understanding of the wars by highlighting the experiences of common soldiers and civilians. As few common soldiers left accounts, their experience is not well known. The experiences of civilians are even more obscure. Nonetheless, a handful of diaries, memoirs, and letters from common soldiers and civilians survive. Several of these rare pieces appear here in English for the first time, including a description of a French *cantinière* (a woman who followed the army selling alcohol and tobacco) and a report about Indian troops in British service. This volume also includes documents written by a German farmer, an Italian noble, and a middle-class French lady. This collection emphasizes the worm's-eye view of the wars as experienced by millions of ordinary people. While campaigns and battles are described, the volume's focus is on daily life and survival. It highlights the human experience at the heart of civil-military interactions during the Napoleonic Wars, such as billeting, foraging, plunder, sexuality, food, illness, religion, and commerce. The complete story of the wars entails much more than fighting; it is the stories about the impact of war that are featured here.

The book begins with an introduction discussing the concept of total war and then lays out the key events of the Napoleonic Wars. Next, it offers a thematic treatment of the main features of the civilian and military experience of Napoleonic warfare: recruitment, conscription, and evasion of service; the formation and nature of military communities; combat and its aftermath; the home front; and demobilization. Each theme is treated comparatively, with attention to Austrian, British, French, Prussian, and Russian particularities. The introduction is followed by a collection of documents that includes four long contemporary accounts (two by soldiers and two by civilians) and five shorter excerpts from both perspectives. Brief headnotes contextualize each document. Presenting French, English, German, Italian, and American voices, both male and female, they offer a broad social and geographic perspective on the Napoleonic Wars.

The documents present an unadorned view of the conflict. The soldiers' memoirs — those of French private Marcellin Marbot (Document 1), British rifleman Benjamin Harris (Document 2), and Württemberg infantryman Jakob Walter (Document 8) — were selected because they describe the full range of military experiences, not just moments of action and glory. Although they fought in major campaigns, battle is not the focus of their memoirs. Rather, their accounts highlight the culture of the military, as well as the struggle against fatigue, hunger, weather, disease, boredom, and fear. These features are also highlighted by the selection of popular images included in the text (Document 6). The fourth military document, a French intelligence report on a mutiny of British colonial troops in India (Document 4), allows a rare glimpse into a non-Western military community during the Napoleonic Wars. Straddling the military-civilian line is the description of Marie Wooden-Head (Document 3), a *cantinière* who accompanied the French army. The *cantinières* were typically uneducated and of modest means, and none is known to have recorded her experiences. The account of Marie Wooden-Head was written by Louis-Gabriel Montigny, an infantry officer in the Grand Army. We chose this document to illustrate the diversity of Napoleonic armies, which included men and women, husbands and wives, parents and children.

The civilian accounts were selected to offer economic, familial, rural, and cosmopolitan points of view on the wars. The letters from William Lee (Document 5), U.S. Consul in Bordeaux, were chosen to highlight the effects of the conflict on Atlantic commerce. We included the excerpt from Roman noble Giovanni Patrizi (Document 7) to delve into the complex emotions of parents when their sons were called up for military service. The diary of Wiesbaden farmer Friederich Ludwig Burk (Document 9) was chosen for its rural perspective on daily life during an unwelcome conflict. Burk seeks to manage his business affairs and maintain normalcy in the face of requisitions, billeting, conscription, looting, and tax increases. He cares little whether the soldiers passing through his life are Austrian or French, Prussian or Russian. The last civilian account is the journal of Julie Pellizzone (Document 10), a highly educated, bourgeois lady of Marseille. This excerpt from her journal is included to provide an explicitly political account of the civil strife produced by economic hardship, regime changes, factionalism, and foreign occupation. Together, the documents open multiple perspectives on the key points of contact between soldiers and civilians during the Napoleonic Wars. They are followed by a chronology of major events, a list of questions for consideration, a selected bibliography, and an index.

A NOTE ABOUT THE TEXTS

Our choice of texts reflects the dearth of sources produced by ordinary soldiers and civilians during the Napoleonic Wars. From among the limited number of existing documents, we have put together a collection intended to offer as many different voices as possible. Our translations seek to retain the flavor of the original texts while making them accessible to contemporary readers. In the case of the journal of Julie Pellizzone, a woman with literary talent, this was relatively simple. It was not an easy task, however, when translating the memoir of foot soldier Jakob Walter or the diary of farmer Friederich Ludwig Burk. Neither man had much education, and neither wrote with the kind of literary flare displayed by Pellizzone. Moreover, they wrote in regional German dialects that occasionally proved difficult to translate. Burk frequently employed local technical terms for crops, currency, and measurements, for example. To make the texts more readable, we chose to translate the more obscure words into simpler language. Unless otherwise noted, all translations are our own.

ACKNOWLEDGMENTS

We thank Lynn Hunt for supporting this project and the editors at Bedford/St. Martin's for their guidance. We thank especially Mary Dougherty, Heidi Hood, Jennifer Jovin, and developmental editor Debra Michals. Thanks as well to the panel of outside readers for their comments and suggestions: Amy Forbes, Millsaps College; Christine Haynes, University of North Carolina, Charlotte; Rob Lewis, Grinnell

College; Alexander Mikaberidze, Louisiana State University, Shreveport; Stephen Miller, University of Alabama, Birmingham; and Frederick Schneid, High Point University. Friends and colleagues have also helped us with this work. Götz Ahrendt, Thomas Cardoza, Gabriele and Lukas Clemens, Denise Davidson, Alan Forrest, Janet Hartley, David Hopkin, Michael Leggiere, Alexander Mizerkabidzhe, Jane Rendall, Christopher Schmidt-Nowara, and Frederick Schneid provided us with primary sources, helped us navigate the secondary literature, suggested images, and read parts of our first draft. We especially thank Tarah Luke and Maureen MacCleod for converting the texts into electronic format and helping identify images.

Rafe Blaufarb
Claudia Liebeskind

Contents

PART ONE

Introduction: An Age of Total War?

War was central to the revolutionary and Napoleonic era. Except for the fourteen-month Peace of Amiens in 1802–1803, much of Europe was at war from 1792 to 1815. The intensity of conflict peaked during Napoleon's reign (1799–1815). In these years, millions of men became soldiers, fought, and died in Europe and around the world. The survivors' wartime encounters with unfamiliar people, distant places, strange cultures, and extreme situations were transformative. Returning veterans related what they had seen and done to wide-eyed audiences in villages they had left years before. Some published memoirs about their experiences, the first time in Western history that ordinary soldiers had done so. Many of these accounts emphasized battle, but the Napoleonic war experience was not restricted to combat. Nor was it reserved for soldiers. The Napoleonic Wars shook the lives of men, women, and children everywhere. Conscription touched families in remote villages, taxes drained their resources, and economic upheaval altered traditional ways of life. In areas where soldiers marched and fought, occupation, rape, pillage, requisition, and disease left lasting scars.

Contemporaries felt that warfare itself had assumed a new form during the Napoleonic period. "Formerly . . . one battled with moderation and consideration according to the conventional proprieties," wrote Napoleonic-era officer Carl von Clausewitz. "The war of the present time is a war of all against all. It is not the King who wars on a king, not an army which wars on an army, but a people which wars on another."[1] Historians have called this "total war" and have defined it as both the unprecedented mobilization of human, material, and psychological forces and as a new understanding of the nature of armed conflict. During the eighteenth century, sovereigns had fought over limited objectives (a town or a province) and had made peace just as readily as they went to war. Battles were waged by relatively small professional armies officered by nobles who viewed warfare as a means to display their courage and generosity. Because of its aristocratic ethos, eighteenth-century warfare was referred to at the time as "war in laces"—a reference to the opulent uniforms soldiers and officers wore. Today, many military historians still consider the 1700s as an age of limited war.

The French Revolution of 1789 began a chain of events that led to a global conflict that transformed the nature of warfare into what has come to be called "total war." The causes of the French revolutionary wars were complex. Revolutionary policies alienated traditionally privileged groups in French society, particularly large sectors of the Catholic Church and aristocracy. The Revolution's efforts to reduce the king's power angered royalists. Outside of France, the crowned heads of Europe were dismayed by the Revolution's increasingly radical policies regarding established religion, social hierarchy, and monarchical government. Several foreign powers, notably the Austrians, began to make threats against France.

Against this international backdrop of saber rattling, domestic politics in France were becoming increasingly polarized. By the beginning of 1792, both the left and the right came to believe that war with the monarchies of Europe would help their respective causes. The left, seeking to overthrow the king and create a republic, believed that war would unmask royalist traitors and bring down the monarchy. The right, in contrast, was confident that the disorganized revolutionary armies would be defeated and that the victorious European powers would restore the throne. With left-right agreement on the need for war, France opened hostilities in April 1792 and within months was facing a European coalition of conservative powers. To confront it, the revolutionaries enacted radical military reforms that transformed the nature of warfare.

The first changes involved conscription, mass armies, and ideological appeals to elicit popular commitment to the war effort. Some appeals were traditional, such as religion (which had featured in earlier conflicts like the Crusades and the Thirty Years' War), and others were new, such as

---

[1] Cited in David A. Bell, *The First Total War: Napoleon's Europe and the Birth of Warfare as We Know It* (Boston: Houghton Mifflin, 2007), 241.

patriotism and democracy. Universal manhood conscription, in particular, represented a sharp break from the voluntary recruitment of professional soldiers during the eighteenth century and made possible the creation of much larger armies of citizen-soldiers. The second shift, the new way of seeing warfare, viewed conflict between nations in uncompromising terms, as an apocalyptic struggle that had to result in absolute victory or total defeat. Wars were recast as fights to the death in which lines between soldier and civilian were blurred. Contemporary evidence—from British caricatures portraying Napoleon as Antichrist to Spanish calls for holy war against the French—suggests that some viewed the Napoleonic Wars in this way, or at least wanted others to do so.

But how much do propaganda and official pronouncements accurately reflect what ordinary soldiers and civilians thought about war? Evidence from the diaries and memoirs of contemporaries suggests that soldiers may have cared more about food and shelter than ideology (Documents 2, 6, and 8), civilians more about commerce, crops, and taxes than patriotism (Documents 5, 9, and 10). On the other hand, it is clear that the Napoleonic Wars featured much larger armies fighting much bloodier battles than during the previous century. Although soldiers and civilians continued to be concerned with the ordinary aspects of daily life and survival, they now inhabited a world in which wars were more uncompromising, ideologies more sharply differentiated, and aims more far-reaching.

THE REVOLUTIONARY AND NAPOLEONIC WARS, 1792–1815

In 1792 revolutionary France declared war on Austria. Within a year, other European monarchies had joined the crusade against the Revolution. In 1793 France responded with the levy-in-mass—a one-time, massive call-up of military manpower and civilian mobilization. By 1794 French armies numbering 750,000 men had thwarted invasion and were poised to attack. It was only in 1796, however, when a young French general named Napoleon Bonaparte led his army into Austrian-dominated Northern Italy, that the tide of war turned decisively in France's favor. A series of victories took Bonaparte to the gates of Vienna in 1797 and resulted in a treaty (the Peace of Campoformio) that knocked Austria out of the war and made the general a national hero. Partly to sideline him, the French government ordered him to invade Egypt. His army arrived there in 1798 and defeated the Mamelukes, slave-soldiers who ruled Egypt for the Ottoman Empire. But victory was ephemeral. A British fleet sunk the ships of the French expedition, stranding Bonaparte's army. The Egyptian population began guerrilla resistance. Sensing that the expedition was doomed, concerned for his reputation, and worried about the situation in France, Bonaparte abandoned his army, eluded the British blockade, and returned home. There, he joined politicians plotting to overthrow the government. On November 9, 1799, their so-called Brumaire coup installed a new government, the Consulate, dominated by Bonaparte.

France was still fighting Great Britain, and Austria had reentered the fray. In May 1800 Bonaparte led an army into Italy, where he defeated the Austrians at the Battle of Marengo (June 14, 1800). In 1801 the Austrians signed the Treaty of Lunéville and left the war. Lacking continental allies, the British felt isolated and signed the Treaty of Amiens with France in 1802. After ten years of war, Europe was at peace. Bonaparte used the respite to consolidate power and prepare for renewed warfare. In 1802 he tried, but failed, to reconquer Haiti, a former French colony whose slave inhabitants had revolted and won freedom. He also asserted French power in Europe. This worried Britain, which reopened hostilities in 1803.

In 1804 Bonaparte, now ruling France as Emperor Napoleon and with Spain as an ally, prepared to invade Britain. He assembled a vast force, the Grand Army, on the Channel coast. Napoleon drilled the army and encouraged its pride with distinctive uniforms, flags, and decorations. It was a motivated, powerful force of trained veterans. Fearing French might, Russia and Austria allied with Britain in 1805. On learning this, Napoleon led the Grand Army against Austria. His troops defeated the Austrians at Ulm (October 20, 1805) before the Russians arrived. The next day, however, the British sank the Franco-Spanish fleet at Trafalgar, destroying Napoleon's naval power. The Russians now joined the Austrians. Although outnumbered, the Grand Army won the Battle of Austerlitz (December 2, 1805) and forced Austria to make peace. Russia, however, kept fighting and was reinforced by Prussia in 1806. Before they could link up, the French attacked. On October 14, 1806, they defeated the Prussians at Jena and Auerstadt. This effectively removed Prussia from the war. On February 8, 1807, the Russians and French fought the Battle of Eylau. Bloody and indecisive, it was followed a few months later by the Battle of Friedland (June 14, 1807). There the Grand Army defeated a smaller Russian force, leading Russia to come to terms. On July 7, 1807, France and Russia signed the Peace of Tilsit. Two days later, France signed a separate treaty with Prussia.

France's only remaining enemy was Britain. Although it could not be attacked directly, Napoleon thought perhaps its economy could be destroyed by embargo. With the Berlin Decree (1806) and the Milan Decree (1807), Napoleon instituted the Continental System banning European trade with Britain (Document 5). Portugal and Spain, however, ignored the ban. To stop this, French troops invaded in October 1807 and made Napoleon's brother, Joseph, king of Spain. Many Spaniards rejected Joseph's rule and started guerrilla resistance (Document 6). British troops landed in Portugal and helped fight the French (Document 2). Although Napoleon's soldiers poured into the Iberian Peninsula, they could never overcome the challenge of waging guerrilla war while also confronting a regular army. The result was a bloody stalemate that gradually slid toward defeat. In 1813 the French were expelled.

Austria saw in Spanish resistance an opportunity to strike the French. Raising the standard of German nationalism and forming a citizens' militia (Landwehr), it moved against France in 1809. The French struck back. They captured Vienna but were checked at Aspern-Essling (May 21–22, 1809). After reinforcing, they attacked again, winning a victory at the Battle of Wagram (July 5–6, 1809) and forcing the Austrians to sue for peace. Napoleon demanded and received permission to wed the Austrian emperor's daughter, Marie-Louise. France was at the height of its power, but new troubles loomed.

At the end of 1810, Russia quit the Continental System. Napoleon decided to invade. In the summer of 1812, he attacked with a 600,000-man multinational army (Document 8). The Russians initially retreated. As the French advanced, they suffered from hunger, fatigue, disease, and the elements. On September 7, 1812, the Russians stood to fight at Borodino, seventy-five miles west of Moscow. The battle was bloody but indecisive. Although the French took Moscow, the Russians refused to surrender. Instead, they burned Moscow to deprive the French of shelter. As winter approached, Napoleon ordered withdrawal. The retreat was catastrophic. The cold killed thousands, and the Russians harassed Napoleon's troops (Document 6). Some of Napoleon's foreign contingents (notably Prussia's) switched sides. Austria followed suit in 1813. Only 100,000 of the original invasion force survived.

In 1813 Russian, Prussian, and Austrian armies allied and closed in for the kill. Scraping together a hastily conscripted army, Napoleon attacked. The French were outnumbered 400,000 to 600,000. In October, the allies cornered the French at Leipzig and fought the Battle of Nations. Lasting three days (October 16–19, 1813), the fighting inflicted heavy losses on the French and drove them from Germany (Document 9). The allies pursued them into France. The French mounted a strong defense but succumbed to superior numbers. Napoleon abdicated on April 6, 1814, and was exiled to the Mediterranean island of Elba. The Congress of Vienna, a conference of the victorious powers, met in September 1814 to discuss the post-Napoleonic European order. This, however, was not the end. On February 25, 1815, Napoleon returned to France and regained power, beginning a short-lived period of rule known as the Hundred Days. Civil war flared up in many parts of the country between Napoleon's supporters and opponents, a struggle called the White Terror (Document 10). The allies sent their armies against him. Napoleon struck first, hoping to defeat them piecemeal. The French army drove back the Prussians at Ligny in Belgium on June 16, 1815. It then attacked the Duke of Wellington's Anglo-Dutch army at Waterloo two days later. But Wellington repulsed the French attacks. Napoleon knew he had lost and returned to Paris. He abdicated on June 22 and was exiled to the South Atlantic island of St. Helena. He died there in 1821.

RECRUITMENT AND EVASION

It was through military recruitment that young men left civilian life and became soldiers. How soldiers were recruited determined the composition and ethos of the different armies of the Napoleonic era. Each country's distinctive recruitment system also reflected key characteristics of its government and people. Finally, recruitment constituted (along with taxes) the main point of contact between state and society during the Napoleonic period. Wherever practiced, one historian has noted, conscription became "the battleground, the ultimate contest of wills between individuals and local communities on the one hand, and a distant impersonal state on the other."[2] Military recruitment could produce resistant civilians, as well as obedient soldiers.

France introduced annual conscription in 1798 when the manpower mobilized by the levy-in-mass had been exhausted. Disease, desertion, combat, and retirement had reduced army strength from its 1794 high of 750,000 to 350,000. To rebuild its army, France adopted a conscription law that, with minor modifications, Napoleon used until his fall (Document 6). According to the law, all Frenchmen aged twenty to twenty-five were subject to military service for five years in peacetime, but for an unlimited period in wartime. Each year the government determined

---

[2] Isser Woloch, "Napoleonic Conscription: State Power and Civil Society," *Past and Present*, no. 111 (May 1986): 101.

the number of conscripts to be raised and assigned each locality part of the total. All eligible young men in the area were to appear before a draft board, which would examine their physical condition, treat exemption requests, and draw lots to determine who would be inducted. Although conscription was bitterly resented, it mustered 2.5 million potential recruits, of whom 1.5 million actually became soldiers. In comparison, only 52,000 men volunteered during Napoleon's rule (Document 1). Conscription was the foundation of France's war effort.

Although it furnished many soldiers, French conscription did not produce an army that exactly reflected the social composition of the nation. In part this was because conscripts who were able to hire replacements could avoid service. Consequently, the wealthy were underrepresented in the army. However, the burden of military service fell upon the whole empire. By 1810 Napoleon had annexed present-day Belgium, Holland, Northern and Western Germany, Northern and Central Italy, parts of Switzerland, and Dalmatia. Hundreds of thousands of young men from these lands were conscripted. Those from elite families were sometimes forced to enter French military schools and become officers—a way of attaching them to Napoleon's empire by giving them prestigious positions in it (Document 7). Military units from satellite states also served in Napoleon's armies. These included the Republic (later Kingdom) of Italy, the Kingdom of Naples, the Kingdom of Spain, and several German states (Documents 8 and 9). Finally, Napoleon was aided by allied independent nations—some enthusiastic like the Poles, others reluctant like the Prussians—which increased the diversity of the Imperial armies. This internationalism culminated in the Russian campaign, in which half of Napoleon's soldiers were not French.

Although the lack of national homogeneity characteristic of the French and most other European armies would today be considered a weakness, at the time national identities were embryonic at best. Most Europeans living in Napoleonic times probably identified more closely with smaller units—typically families, villages, and provinces—or larger ones, notably the Catholic Church or one of the multinational empires such as the Austrian or British. Nationality was less important to fighting capacity than it is today. Over the course of the Napoleonic Wars, however, national identity may have become more important to military effectiveness as combatant countries like Prussia increasingly appealed to patriotism to stimulate their troops' energies. The Napoleonic Wars were thus part of the historical process by which Europeans came to identify themselves in national terms over the course of the nineteenth century.

The armies fighting the French Empire were mainly recruited by traditional methods. These, however, differed from country to country, reflecting the distinctive characteristics of each. Napoleon's most persistent foe, Austria, used diverse methods to recruit the different nationalities of its multinational empire. In the reliable German and Bohemian heartlands, a form of conscription was used. But in Northern Italy, Tyrol, and Polish Galicia, it was feared that conscription might awaken separatism and inspire a rebellion. There, recruitment was voluntary. A third area was Hungary, a technically independent kingdom exempt from military service in the Austrian armies. Hungary did, however, provide volunteers—including the Insurrectio, a quasi-feudal force. The final recruitment zone was Austria's border with the Ottoman Empire. Populated by militarily organized Serbs and Croats, this region furnished special Grenzer (border-guard) regiments.

The British Army was also heterogeneous, albeit for different reasons. Theoretically voluntary, it attracted men on the margins of society who saw military service as an attractive alternative to jail or destitution. To fill the ranks, recruiters forcibly enrolled men or tricked them into signing up, often by plying them with drink (Document 2). Many soldiers were recruited in the British Isles, but large numbers were international mercenaries and adventurers. At various times, Britain fielded regiments of Hanoverians, French émigrés, Sicilians, Maltese, Greeks, Portuguese, and Spanish. Only half of Wellington's troops at Waterloo were British. The international character of Britain's army was especially pronounced in its colonies. Most British troops in the West Indies were of African descent, including slaves serving to obtain freedom. In India the sepoys (colonial troops) came from various religions and ethnicities (Document 4). Unfortunately, few indigenous soldiers from the colonial units left letters, diaries, or memoirs, so we know little of their experiences. During the Napoleonic Wars, Britain also formed voluntary home-defense units (Document 2). Known variously as militia, fencibles, yeomen, and volunteers, these units never saw combat because France could not invade Britain.

Before its crushing defeat in 1807, Prussia recruited its army in two ways: by conscripting natives and by hiring foreign mercenaries. Theoretically, all Prussians were liable to conscription. In practice, however, there were many exemptions. Towns, like Berlin, and certain regions, like the Duchy of Cleves, were spared because of special arrangements they had with the crown. Also, people deemed economically indispensable were not conscripted: businessmen, skilled workers, landowners, fathers, sons of widows, cooks, gardeners, and apprentices. Moreover, conscripts spent only two months annually with the army. The rest of the year, they worked at home. The Prussian monarchy viewed its subjects as irreplaceable economic resources. It preferred recruiting foreign mercenaries, who constituted half of the army. Prussian recruiters scoured Europe, enlisting all sorts of people, but principally Austrians, Germans, Swiss, French, and Italians. Although conscription gave Prussia the potential for creating a more national force, it did not pursue this course until after 1807, when it began an intensive program of military modernization. Until then, its preference for mercenaries made its army as international as those of France, Austria, and Britain.

Russia's army was the most homogeneous of the period. Although it mobilized some Central Asian tribesmen, most of its soldiers were ethnic Russians. They were recruited by a conscription system in which each village contributed a quota of men annually. The system was administered locally by village elites, who usually designated the poorer inhabitants for service. Those chosen were unfortunate indeed. Until 1793, service was for life; thereafter, it was for twenty-five years. The chance of a recruit's returning home was so remote that villages held symbolic funerals for departing conscripts. The military thus formed a society separate from the nation, but paradoxically, it was more national in composition than the other Napoleonic armies.

Repeated defeats from 1800 to 1809 put pressure on Napoleon's adversaries to reform their military systems. The temptation was great, as the king of Prussia put it, to make "our army more like the French."[3] Yet the risks were also great. Many conservatives feared that adopting French methods would unleash revolutionary forces by mobilizing and arming the masses. Britain and Russia, which both emerged relatively unscathed from their encounters with Napoleon, rejected reform. But Austria and Prussia, which had suffered disastrous defeats, opted for change. Austrian reforms were less profound than those of Prussia. They were limited to the creation in 1808 of the Landwehr, a citizens' militia, and appeals to German nationalism when war with France resumed in 1809. The Landwehr fought well, but it was too small to save Austria. The calls for a German national rising against the French fell on deaf ears. Prussia's reforms, begun after its defeat in 1807, were more serious. They consisted in opening the officer corps to talent, creating a system of reserves, and forming militias, which included units of well-off volunteers (Jägers), a Landwehr, and a Landsturm. The latter was a nonuniformed

[3] Cited in Gunther E. Rothenberg, *The Art of Warfare in the Age of Napoleon* (Bloomington: Indiana University Press, 1978), 189.

reserve that was never activated. The Jägers and Landwehr, however, served in the final campaigns against Napoleon. These military efforts were seconded by nationalistic propaganda calling for a war of German liberation against the French. After 1815, the reforms were rolled back and the rhetoric toned down—but not forgotten.

Along with taxes, military service was the most hated obligation imposed by Napoleonic-era states. The departure of a son for the army could spell financial ruin for a family that needed his labor on the farm. Thus the efforts of people to avoid conscription—and the state's efforts to enforce it—constituted a contentious chapter in the evolution of state-society relations. But not everybody had difficulty avoiding the draft. Many were excused because they failed to meet the army's physical standards (Document 9). One-third of the 2.5 million Frenchmen called before a draft board were rejected because they were too short, lacked teeth, had poor eyesight or hearing, or suffered from illness.

The physically fit could still avoid the draft since only a percentage of eligible recruits were actually inducted. Those with a high number could feel confident they would remain untouched. But those who drew a low number knew they would have to act to avoid service. Those with money could purchase the services of a replacement—generally a young man without property whose absence would not affect his family's economic welfare too adversely. In France, the rate of replacement was at least 4.5 percent, and in certain areas it reached 30 percent. As more and more replacements were sought during the course of the war, their price rose—as much as sevenfold between 1800 and 1815.[4] Those who offered themselves as replacements could bring substantial financial benefits to their families, perhaps saving them from crushing debt. The practice of replacement was found wherever military service was obligatory.

Unwilling conscripts too poor to afford a replacement had to take more drastic steps to avoid service. Some resorted to self-mutilation, knocking out the teeth used to tear open cartridges or maiming their trigger fingers. Others drank concoctions intended to produce temporary symptoms of illness. An unknown number bribed doctors to issue false certificates of unfitness. Matrimony offered another way to avoid service since married men were exempt. The approach of the conscription season could produce a crop of marriages, often between young men and elderly widows who were no longer virgins, were beyond childbearing years, and

---

[4] Woloch, "Napoleonic Conscription," 113–17. Replacement prices increased from 1,000 to 7,000 francs.

who often needed extra money. In France, the Revolution's legalization of divorce allowed such unions to be repeated again and again.

The most common form of draft avoidance was evasion. Many young men refused to appear before the draft board, instead hiding with friends or family or fleeing to woods, swamps, or mountains. Draft evaders were often hidden and given work by their communities. They were local boys after all, and a cheap source of labor. It was only through multiple methods of coercion—the billeting (lodging) of troops with evaders' families, police investigations, military sweeps, and fines on the richest villagers—that Napoleon finally broke the will of his empire's inhabitants and forced them to accept obligatory military service.

For young men who had been inducted, there was one final means of evasion: desertion. New conscripts were prone to desert while traveling to the army, before entering the military community. All governments took steps to ensure that draftees actually reached the army. In the French Empire, conscripts were marched off in groups under military escort and given military training on the way to the front. Russia employed a lighter touch. Conscripts were led to the army by officers who eased them into military life. Their daily marches were only half as long as those of seasoned troops, they took frequent breaks, and the escorting officer introduced them only gradually to drill and discipline. Regardless of nationality, once conscripts reached their regiments, desertion rates declined. In part this was because the deserter's prospects were not good. Alone and unable to speak the local language, he was isolated and vulnerable. He was at the mercy not only of the military police but also of peasants who regarded passing soldiers with distrust—as potential plunderers, rapists, and murderers. Moreover, many soldiers, particularly in the long-service armies of Napoleon's enemies, had no civilian lives to return to because they had been gone for so long. Many who did desert, therefore, turned to crime, forming gangs with up to fifty members. Conscription was not only a major means of military recruitment, but also a significant source of criminality.

THE MILITARY COMMUNITY

When a conscript joined his regiment, he entered an unfamiliar world, a military community distinct from the civilian one he had left. For many, the experience was transformative. Most armies developed rituals to consecrate the conscript's break with the civilian world, underline his new identity, and develop a sense of group loyalty. European armies issued elaborate uniforms to soldiers, visibly demarcating them from civilians. In the French army, soldiers received military nicknames (for example, Pretty Flower and Drinks without Thirst). Certain units required soldiers to grow distinctive mustaches and wear their hair in special styles (Document 1). In Russia, for example, recruits had their heads and beards shaved, a practice that replaced the previous method of distinguishing soldiers—branding with a red-hot iron. Upon entering the army, moreover, they literally acquired a new legal status. In their villages, they had been serfs. As soldiers, they shed the stigma of serfdom and became free men. In the British army, recruits were taught regimental lore and were encouraged to see themselves as part of a distinctive, historical community. In all armies, pride in one's unit and traditions were powerful sources of personal identity formation, group cohesion, and fighting effectiveness.

For recruits, the military community was a tough world. Repeated drilling, the routine of guard duty, the culture of hierarchical obedience, the violent disciplinary regime, the boredom—all combined to create a lifestyle different from that of the village or urban workshop. The military community also featured strange people, many of whom were foreign, and unaccustomed values, notably a hypermasculinized culture of honor. For some recruits, army life meant freedom and adventure, especially in the sexual sphere, unobtainable in the stifling world of the village. But for others, excitement was overshadowed by loneliness. Young peasants who had never left home before often experienced profound homesickness. Today we would consider this clinical depression, and like depression, it could result in reduced disease resistance and even death from suicide and other causes. Homesickness was the principal cause of desertion. To fight feelings of homesickness, soldiers sought friendships with comrades from their own region (Document 8). They also wrote home, seeking news of familiar things—the harvest, family finances, friends, sweethearts. Although they often expressed pride at being soldiers, many also urged their parents to find replacements for their younger brothers. Soldiers' feelings about military life varied widely from man to man, and a single soldier could have multiple, contrasting emotions at the same time.

The military community was not exclusively male. Women and children formed an important part of the army's population, both in garrison and on campaign. All armies allowed a certain number of soldiers' wives and children to be carried on the regimental rolls and officially authorized to accompany the army (Documents 2–4). Although the exact quota varied, it was usually between six and eight wives per 100 soldiers.

There were many more military women without official status. Because they were not registered, their numbers are unknown. All of these women—registered and unregistered—performed key functions for the armies. They provided companionship and sex as wives, unmarried partners, and prostitutes. They also worked for the regiments, particularly laundering and doing needlework, and often performed heavy labor. To the sick and wounded, they served as nurses. Some were shrewd entrepreneurs who set up profitable businesses selling food, alcohol, and tobacco to the soldiers. Known as *cantinières* or *vivandières* in the French army, they erected huts or tents where they plied their trade (Document 3). These became centers of military sociability where soldiers spent leisure time. Military women were also critical to the plunder economy of the army. They not only pillaged and looted themselves, but they also served as intermediaries, buying pilfered goods from the soldiers and reselling them. Finally, army women bore and raised children. Their sons were thought to make fine future soldiers, so formal positions were established for them. They received pay, rations, and basic instruction. Although military women and children were usually noncombatants, they faced the dangers and hardships of military life: boredom, fatigue, hunger, cold, disease, violence, and death. Unfortunately, no military women published memoirs. Our knowledge of their experience comes from secondhand accounts of soldiers and civilians (Documents 2–4 and 10).

Even when in garrison, soldiers' living conditions were difficult. Where they existed, barracks were dank and ill-lit. With soldiers sleeping several to a bed, disease was rampant. Along with being unhealthy, garrison life was psychologically trying. Days were filled with drills and long spells of sentry duty. Although the constant activity was intended to keep soldiers from becoming listless and demoralized, the endless repetition of mindless routines may have had the opposite effect. Discipline was harsh and punishment usually corporal (whippings and beatings). While infrequent, executions of soldiers for crimes like murder and desertion were dramatic and public (Document 2). Carried out before assembled soldiers, they were intended to make an unforgettable impression.

When soldiers were not involved in their military occupations, they often worked in town, perhaps plying trades they had learned before entering the army. French and British soldiers supplemented their pay in this way. In Russia—where, despite the formal change in soldiers' status, relations between officers and men resembled those between lords and serfs—soldiers had to work for their superiors. In some cases, officers leased their soldiers' labor to civilians.

Military life was hard, but not all was boredom, deprivation, and exploitation. Soldiers still found leisure time, which they generally spent with their male and female comrades—drinking, smoking, gambling, and singing—often around a campfire or in a *cantinière*'s tent (Document 3). During the Napoleonic era, armies were frequently on the move, the French most of all (Document 8). When in no hurry, French troops marched ten to twelve miles per day, at a rate of three miles per hour, with frequent breaks. But in the heat of a campaign, they might march up to thirty-five miles. While on campaign, soldiers generally preferred spending their nights billeted in civilian homes—to the distress of their occupants (Documents 2, 8, and 9). When necessary, they slept in tents or in the open.

Marching soldiers lived in small groups that foraged and cooked together in a common kettle (Documents 2, 6, and 8). In the Russian army, these groups were called *artels* and numbered about ten soldiers. In France, these groups, *ordinaires*, were slightly larger. The French soldier's official daily ration during the 1805 campaign was one and a half pounds of bread, half a pound of meat, and either one ounce of rice or two ounces of dried fruit. For the soldiers in this campaign, which featured legendary forced marches and some of the fiercest combat of the era, this was inadequate. Armies on campaign often outstripped their army's supply service and went hungry. When this happened, they requisitioned supplies from civilians, offering official IOUs for what they took. Requisitioning easily slipped into pillaging. Soldiers usually engaged in pillaging to make up for supply shortfalls (Document 6). For example, British troops in the Iberian Peninsula were so poorly supplied that they had to pillage to feed themselves (Document 2). But many soldiers also pillaged for profit, selling their take to military women, peddlers, and civilians. Some soldiers may have even pillaged for fun (Document 1).

Civilians feared soldiers (Documents 6 and 9). Even regulated requisitioning embittered them because it deprived them of real assets in exchange for papers promising reimbursement. Pillaging was worse. Soldiers' reputation for marauding and theft was so strong that civilians made scant distinction between friends and foes. Like their early modern forebears, the peasantry of Napoleonic Europe viewed all soldiers, regardless of nationality, as a threat. The practice of billeting passing troops in civilian homes sharpened their hostility (Documents 9 and 10). Billeted soldiers required food, firewood, and bedding. If they were not satisfied with what their hosts provided, they often took what they wanted or felt they deserved. Theft and vandalism were common, as were seduction and rape (Document 2). Resistance to the soldiers' demands invited violence. Yet what civilians feared most about soldiers—their predatory behavior and lack of restraint—could also inspire envy. Free from civilian moral constraints, endowed with power and mobility, soldiers incarnated a lifestyle that appealed to the restless and adventurous.

The wars caused a great movement of people that exposed millions of individuals—civilians and soldiers, non-Europeans and Europeans—to new cultures. The range of soldiers' encounters with the unfamiliar was wide. In the French army, soldiers served across the European continent, from Portugal to Russia, as well as overseas in Egypt and Haiti. British soldiers were even greater globe-trotters, serving in Canada and the Caribbean, Africa and the Mediterranean, and South Asia, as well as on the European continent. Even Russia's purely continental campaigns exposed its soldiers to a world they otherwise could have never imagined. What caught the soldiers' eye ranged from the mundane (different ways of laying out villages, growing crops, and building houses) to the sublime (a first glimpse of the sea, a mountain, a city, or a palace) (Document 8).

As they encountered Catholics, Protestants, Orthodox Christians, Jews, or Muslims for the first time, soldiers also grappled with religious diversity (Document 2). Although some were indifferent to the religious practices they encountered and others moved by them, still others lashed out at faiths they regarded as heresy. "Since leaving Frankfurt," wrote a Catholic French soldier in Germany, "I have not found any true Christians. . . . There are only Protestants."[5] Jewish civilians received particularly bad treatment, including verbal and physical abuse, theft, vandalism, and murder. Civilians experienced a comparable pageant of ethnic, religious, and linguistic diversity as the armies crisscrossed the continent (Document 9). Even if the resulting interactions sometimes reinforced existing stereotypes, they led to unprecedented cross-cultural contact.

COMBAT AND ITS AFTERMATH

What kept soldiers in the army, enduring suffering and want? What impelled them forward into battle, to face grievous injury, mutilation, or death? How did they cope with their dangerous and stressful situation? To a great extent, fear of the harsh punishments meted out for

---

[5] Cited in Alan Forrest, *Napoleon's Men: The Soldiers of the Revolution and Empire* (London: Hambledon, 2002), 111.

disobedience, cowardice, and desertion kept soldiers in line. The lack of better opportunities in the civilian world also kept many soldiers from abandoning the military. Political ideology may have also played a motivational role, especially in the armies of revolutionary France. During the 1790s, French government propaganda sought to "revolutionize" the troops. Napoleonic propaganda shifted focus, emphasizing military glory and the cult of personality Napoleon fostered rather than political themes (Document 3). It is unclear to what extent either effort influenced the soldiers or how they interpreted the messages they received. Many soldiers were skeptical. For example, Napoleon's military newspaper, the *Bulletin of the Grand Army*, was called *Le Menteur* (The Liar) by the soldiers because it habitually reported defeats as victories. Most soldiers, even the French, were apolitical. Many, however, were religious, which helped them cope with the ever-present threat of death. In the armies fighting France, moreover, religion was deliberately employed in a motivational role. Napoleon's enemies used religious imagery and rhetoric to demonize him and discredit his cause (Document 7). In Spain and Russia, the clergy mobilized popular resistance against Napoleon. In Prussia during the final years of war, the Landwehr sometimes marched into battle singing Protestant hymns. But not all armies in the anti-French coalition cast their cause in religious terms. Among British troops, excessive piety was ridiculed as unmanly, suggesting that notions of masculinity also played a role in military motivation.

Along with political and religious factors, other sources of motivation were pride in the unit, devotion to leaders, ambition, and comradeship. Pride in one's military unit was encouraged and deliberately instilled in all armies (Documents 1 and 2). Each regiment wore a distinctive uniform and went into battle with its own regimental flags. In the French army, these listed the battles in which the unit had fought. To lose a flag was a great source of shame. Revered leaders could also inspire valor. Napoleon set the standard in this regard. Through deliberate gestures—from mass ceremonies to the distribution of tobacco to soldiers the night before battle—Napoleon cultivated an image that was simultaneously illustrious, heroic, and human. His effect on the soldiers was electrifying. According to Wellington, Napoleon's presence on the battlefield was worth 50,000 men. Other leaders, including the Russian general Alexander Suvorov and some of Napoleon's marshals, had similar effects.

Soldiers also strove for promotion and decorations. Although all European armies granted officers' commissions to exceptionally talented soldiers, they discriminated against those without wealth or pedigree. The French army was different. The Revolution had opened careers to talent in 1789, and despite Napoleon's attempts to reimpose a degree of social exclusiveness, the officer corps remained open to talent through 1815. Seventy-five percent of Napoleon's officers began their careers as soldiers. Desire for promotion, which brought money and social status, had a powerful impact on French military motivation. In addition to this, Napoleon instituted a decoration, the Legion of Honor, to reward bravery. He also created a merit-based noble status that he bestowed on officers. All this helped motivate the army. However, it was probably comradeship that was decisive in keeping the armies fighting. The desire to protect one's buddies—those with whom one marched, ate, and slept—led Napoleonic-era soldiers (like their descendants in later wars) to ignore their safety and risk their lives.

For soldiers, the climax of the military experience was the battle (Documents 2 and 8). Napoleonic battles involved thousands of soldiers, who fought using elaborate formations and maneuvers. Linear formations brought maximum firepower to bear on the enemy but were vulnerable to cavalry attack. To counter mounted charges, infantry lines could redeploy into hollow squares, but these were vulnerable to artillery fire. To attack, infantry could form columns. These densely packed formations, however, were also vulnerable to artillery fire. The art of tactical leadership was to balance the advantages and disadvantages of these different formations and choose the appropriate one for a given situation. To train soldiers to effect rapid battlefield redeployments from line to square to column and back again was the purpose of their interminable drilling. Nonetheless, battlefields inevitably became chaotic. One French soldier described his first experience of battle this way:

> When I first stepped onto the field of carnage, it is difficult to say what I felt seeing my comrades, horses and men knocked head over heels. The numbers of wounded leaving the battle, mutilated, disheveled, carried on stretchers, their faces pale, their bodies covered with dust and blood, the shouts of the dying, the frenzy of fighting men, the collective image of it all troubled my senses in a way that is difficult to define. When I found myself exposed to the enemy artillery batteries, vomiting terror and death into our ranks, I was struck by trembling, but was it fright or dread? . . . I felt ready to faint. . . . But we hurled ourselves at the enemy, and then I no longer felt fear.[6]

Although Napoleonic combat produced some touching examples of humanity toward friend and foe, it was more typically a brutal—and

---

[6] Ibid., 113–14.

brutalizing—experience. Prisoners were often shot in cold blood (Document 8). The dead and wounded were stripped of their possessions, even clothes, by friend, foe, and civilian alike. After battle, the naked corpses were dumped into mass graves by local civilians gathered for that purpose. The stench was appalling.

Although the Napoleonic Wars are famous for their pitched battles, they also featured guerrilla conflict between regular troops and civilian insurgents. Lacking uniforms and eschewing formal tactics, insurgents avoided open-field combat. Instead, they ambushed stragglers, attacked military hospitals, and waylaid supply columns (Document 8). When regular troops arrived, they hid their weapons and resumed their civilian existences or returned to their remote hideouts. In most countries they occupied, French armies met guerrilla resistance. But while the insurgencies in Italy, Tyrol, and Russia were unpleasant, they never reached the scale of the conflict in the Iberian Peninsula. Lasting from 1807 until the expulsion of the French in 1813, that war pinned down hundreds of thousands of Napoleonic troops and cost them about a hundred men a day. In this confused conflict, which combined features of a national uprising, a civil war, anarchy, and regular warfare, combatants practiced unspeakable atrocities. Spanish insurgents routinely tortured French prisoners and mutilated their corpses. The French retaliated in kind, venting their frustration on civilians. The Spanish insurgency was supported by an Anglo-Portuguese army (Document 2). This presented the French with a dilemma: Should they concentrate against the Anglo-Portuguese, or should they spread out their troops to pacify the Spanish countryside? Napoleon never made a clear decision—and lost the war.

The Napoleonic Wars resulted in massive loss of life. Although there are no exact figures, especially for civilians, at least several million people died. As we have seen, battles were murderous affairs in which troops shot each other at short range and artillery decimated the tightly packed ranks of the enemy. The fate of the wounded was grim. Trained doctors, everywhere in short supply, viewed preemptive amputation as the best way to save a wounded soldier's life. After a battle, it was not uncommon to see piles of amputated limbs near the medical tents and makeshift hospitals (Documents 2 and 8). Hospitals were overcrowded, fetid places from which many never returned. As germ theory was unknown and sterilization not practiced, wounds became infected and gangrene was common. Hospitals bred disease, but perhaps no more than the barracks, tents, and civilian houses in which soldiers spent most of their military existence.

Disease was the greatest killer during the Napoleonic Wars. Generally referred to as "fever," diseases common to the wars ranged from yellow fever to dysentery to influenza. The West Indies were notoriously fatal. Between 1793 and 1796, at least 40,000 British soldiers stationed there died of yellow fever and other tropical maladies. But the European theater was deadly too. Of 39,000 British troops landed on Walchern Island (Holland) in July 1809, only 4,000 remained fit for duty when the force was withdrawn the following December. In this disastrous campaign, over 4,000 British soldiers died of "Walchern fever," but only one hundred were killed by enemy action (Document 2). Death from disease was not a British monopoly. In the first five weeks of the Russian campaign, Napoleon's armies lost one-third of their manpower to various maladies. In contrast to battle, however, which killed relatively few noncombatants, disease made no distinction between soldiers and civilians (Document 9). From an epidemiological perspective, the Napoleonic Wars were a vast exchange of deadly microorganisms across Europe. Transmitted not only between soldiers and civilians but also between animals, the wars spread disease to every corner of the continent.

THE HOME FRONT

The Napoleonic Wars touched civilians in many ways, directly and indirectly. Even regions that saw no passing soldiers, where no battles were fought, felt war's impact through conscription, tax increases, and economic disruption. The Napoleonic Wars were not just a military conflict but an economic one too, pitting the industrial and commercial might of Great Britain against that of the French Empire. Through the Continental System, Napoleon sought to choke Britain's overseas trade, ruin its economy, and force it to submit (Documents 5, 9, and 10). Britain retaliated with Orders in Council banning trade with the French Empire. For France, the impact was mixed. Hardship was experienced in some areas of the economy, and there was an almost total absence of colonial goods. Napoleon responded with innovation, for example encouraging the cultivation of sugar beets to replace Caribbean cane. At one point, he even considered replacing his troops' blue uniform with a grayish white garment because of lack of dye, a colonial product. The British blockade hurt France's port cities (Documents 5 and 10) and those in Europe as well. Some enterprising souls on the continent did profit, however, from smuggling with the British. On the level of industry and manufacturing, the impact of economic warfare was cushioned by French domination in Europe, which allowed Napoleon to protect French industries and treat the countries under his sway as a captive market. And, of course, industries manufacturing war material thrived.

In Britain, the Continental System also produced varying results. The textile industries suffered because most of their production had been exported to continental Europe. Some new markets for textiles and manufactured goods were opened in India and Spanish America (Document 4), but these were not enough to absorb British industrial output. Unemployment rose, and calls for peace were heard. Some British elites feared that revolution might break out. But as in France, not all sectors of the economy suffered equally. Some even thrived. Shipbuilding, metallurgy, and other war-related industries naturally did well, but there were some unexpected bright spots too. For example, the domestic manufacturing of straw hats boomed when Italy, Britain's traditional supplier, fell under the Continental System and could no longer export its wares.

LIFE AFTER SERVICE

The Napoleonic Wars made a mark on several generations. Many of the survivors returned with horrible wounds, poor health, and memories that would haunt them for the rest of their days. Even some of those who escaped unscathed experienced trouble reentering civilian life. Most of the Napoleonic-era armies made little provision for the social reinsertion of wounded and elderly soldiers. In Russia, the most extreme example, the country's tradition of conscripting soldiers for life meant that they were not expected to leave the army at all, but rather to die in the service. Aged veterans were kept on the regimental rolls, receiving pay and rations, although not required to perform any military duties. In Prussia, old soldiers who insisted on retiring or whose health and fitness did not permit them to serve anymore were sent away with a beggar's license. The lot of retired veterans was better in Great Britain, where they and their families received small pensions (Document 2).

French veterans enjoyed even better prospects for reentering civilian life or having a dignified military retirement. There are several reasons for this. First, a large percentage of the soldiers demobilized from Napoleon's armies in 1814 and 1815 were recent conscripts (called Marie-Louises after the empress) mobilized after the retreat from Russia. These young veterans had spent only one or two years in the army, had never wanted to become soldiers, and had not yet had time to become fully acculturated into the military milieu. It was with great relief that they returned to their villages, where most were speedily and smoothly reintegrated. Second, the French Revolution had improved the status of soldiers by recasting them as patriotic citizen-heroes. It had set up extensive retirement programs for veterans that allowed old soldiers to collect pensions or live in the national veteran's home in Paris, the Invalides. There, a spirit of egalitarianism prevailed: Soldiers who had lost a limb in combat received officer rank, and the men and officers ate exactly the same food. Although Napoleon reversed some of the Revolution's more egalitarian regulations, life at the Invalides remained good for old soldiers. Napoleon and his successors continued to offer pensions to soldiers who chose to retire to their villages and gave them bonuses (marriage dowries and land) on special occasions.

It is difficult to measure the influence of returning veterans, but it was surely great. Their accounts of faraway places and unfamiliar customs, not to mention their tales of martial glory, must have had an impact on the generation of European youth who grew up in the 1820s (Document 6). As the veterans aged, many began to set down their reminiscences in memoirs. They were the first common soldiers to do so. In the eighteenth century, generals and high-ranking officers had written accounts of their wartime deeds. Now in the mid-nineteenth century, even low-ranking officers and a few common soldiers (especially in England) began to publish their stories. This trend peaked in the 1850s and 1860s, when Napoleon's nephew established a new French empire under the title Napoleon III. Eager to bolster his legitimacy by associating himself with his uncle's glory, Napoleon III encouraged veterans to write about their experiences. Many of these memoirs were unabashedly celebratory and less than convincing. Fortunately, some accounts were not intended as propaganda (Documents 2, 8, 9, and 10).

The Napoleonic Wars not only affected the lives of millions of individuals. They also delivered a rude shock to the established order of monarchical Europe and profoundly influenced the subsequent history of the continent. Although Napoleon had been defeated, Europe would never be the same again. Evidence for this can be seen in the efforts of the victorious powers to guarantee European political stability and stifle revolutionary movements wherever they might occur. Although they had won the military struggle, leaders were extremely nervous about the forces—democracy, nationalism, and total war—that had been unleashed by Revolutionary and Napoleonic France. Through coordinated action beginning with the Congress of Vienna, the conservative monarchies succeeded in maintaining the traditional socio-political order and avoiding war for several decades after 1815. But even these efforts stemmed only temporarily the new ideological currents the Napoleonic Wars had spread across Europe. By the mid-nineteenth century, nationalism and revolution (now in the guise of socialism) had reappeared on a massive scale.

War, too, returned to the European scene in the mid-1850s. Military innovations honed during the Napoleonic Wars (conscription and militaristic appeals to national pride) began to be harnessed to recent technological advances (the railroad, the rifle, and high explosive artillery) to create a truly lethal blend. The devastating potential of the marriage of Napoleonic-style mobilization and modern technology was first demonstrated in the Franco-Prussian War (1870–1871). In that conflict, a much larger, more scientifically advanced, and professionally led Prussian army crushed a French force formed and led along classic Napoleonic lines. A page had been turned. Countries that had previously copied the military model of Napoleonic France now scrambled to follow the Prussian example of technologically organized mass warfare. When Europe went to war in 1914, the result was an unprecedented bloodbath in which conscripted armies of millions slaughtered each other with machine guns, high explosives, poison gas, and aerial bombs. The blending of Napoleonic mass mobilization with nineteenth-century technological and scientific innovation had come to fruition in a truly horrific version of total war.

PART TWO

The Documents

1

GENERAL MARCELLIN MARBOT

Memoirs

1844

Jean-Baptiste-Antoine Marcellin Marbot (1782–1854) was raised in rural France, in the province of Quercy. He came from a noble military family. His father, already an officer before 1789, became a general in the revolutionary wars. Following family tradition, Marcellin joined the army in 1799, just as Bonaparte was taking power. He participated in many of the principal battles of the Napoleonic Wars, winning promotion to the rank of colonel and receiving the title of baron from Napoleon. As a strong supporter of Napoleon's regime, Marbot was banished by the restored Bourbon government in 1815. The revolution of 1830 deposed the Bourbons, and Marbot returned to France. Reinstated in the military with the rank of general, he served with distinction in the French conquest of North Africa (1830s–1840s). In 1844 he set down his recollections of his Napoleonic military experiences for his wife and two sons. Although intended only for his family, his memoir was published more than forty years after his death. In the excerpt translated here, Marbot relates his entry into military service at the tender age of seventeen, detailing the process of becoming a soldier, identifying with and becoming loyal to a unit, and adapting to military life. This excerpt provides a rare glimpse of the distinctive culture of the French army during the transition from revolutionary to Napoleonic rule.

Since there was no longer a military school and since one only entered the army as a simple soldier,[1] my father . . . enrolled me in the 1st Hussar Regiment (formerly known as Bercheny), which was part of the division he was to command in Italy; it was September 3, 1799.

My father took me to the tailor charged with making [uniforms] and ordered me a complete hussar outfit, as well as all arms and equipment,

---

[1] This was an egalitarian reform of the Revolution, which Napoleon quickly undid by restoring direct officer recruitment and military schooling.

General Baron Jean-Baptiste-Antoine Marcellin Marbot, *Mémoires du général baron de Marbot* (Paris, 1891), 1:41–81.

etc. etc. . . . There I was, a soldier! . . . a hussar! . . . My joy was indescribable! . . . But it was troubled when, returning to the hotel, I realized that it was going to worsen the suffering of my brother Adolph, two years older than me and still parked in school like a child! I resolved to tell him of my enrollment only at the same time as announcing that I wanted to spend the month before my departure [for the army] with him. I thus begged my father to let me stay near Adolph . . . until the day when we had to leave for Italy. My father perfectly understood the reason for this request; he granted it to me, and led me the next day back to [school].

Can you imagine my return there? . . . It was recess, and all play suddenly stopped; all the students, young and old, surrounded me. . . . The success of the hussar was complete!

Departure day arrived . . . and I left my mother and three brothers with the greatest pain, despite the pleasure I felt at entering the military career. . . .

The city of Nice[2] was filled with troops, among which was a squadron of the 1st Hussars, to which I belonged. In the absence of its colonel, it was commanded by a very brave squadron leader named Muller (he was the father of the poor adjutant of the 7th Hussars who was wounded by a cannonball near me at Waterloo). Upon learning that the general had just arrived, Commander Muller went to my father, and they agreed that, after several days of rest, I would serve in the 7th company, commanded by Captain Mathis, a man of merit who later became colonel under the Empire and general under the Restoration.

Although my father was very good to me, he intimidated me so much that I was extremely timid around him, a timidity he thought even greater than it really was; thus, he said that I should have been a girl, and he often called me Miss Marcellin: this bothered me greatly, especially since I had become a hussar. It was to overcome this timidity that my father wanted me to perform the same service as my comrades; moreover, as I have already said, one could only enter the army as a simple soldier. It is true that my father could have had me serve directly with him, since my regiment was part of his division; but, beside the reasoning I indicated above, he wanted me to learn how to saddle and bridle my horse, care for my weapons, and did not want his son to enjoy the slightest privilege, which would have produced a bad effect among the troops. It was already enough that I had been admitted to the squadron without having had to endure a long and boring apprenticeship at the depot.

[2] In southeastern France, a staging area for French military operations in Italy.

I spent several days surveying the very beautiful surroundings of Nice with my father and his staff; but the moment for me to enter the squadron having arrived, my father asked Commander Muller to send for Sergeant Pertelay. . . . He arrived and what did we see? A big jolly fellow, immaculate it is true, but with his shako[3] over his ear, his saber dragging, his face red [from drink] and bisected by an immense scar, waxed mustaches half a foot long which disappeared behind his ears, two great tresses on his temples which, emerging from under his shako, hung down to his chest, and with all that, an air!! . . . the air of a bandit, which was augmented by a brusque manner of speaking and by a most barbarous Franco-Alsatian jargon. This last defect did not surprise my father, since he knew that the 1st Hussars was the former Bercheny Regiment, which had previously recruited Germans and where, until 1793, commands were given in German, which was generally used by the officers and hussars, almost all of whom were from the provinces along the Rhine; but my father could not have been more surprised by my mentor's bearing, responses, and duelist-like aura.

I later learned that he had hesitated placing me in the hands of this fellow, but that since . . . the colonel had identified him as the squadron's best noncommissioned officer, my father had decided to try him out. I thus followed Pertelay who, taking me by the arm, led me into my room, showed me how to put my belongings in my chest, and led me to a small barracks in a former convent occupied by the squadron of the 1st Hussars. My mentor had me saddle and unsaddle a pretty little horse that my father had bought me; then he showed me where to put my coat and weapons; finally, he gave me a complete demonstration and decided, once he had explained everything, that it was time to have dinner, for my father, desiring me to eat with my mentor, had given us extra pay for that expense.

Pertelay led me into a small inn filled with hussars, grenadiers, and soldiers of all branches. We were served, and an enormous bottle of the most violent harsh red wine was placed on the table, from which Pertelay poured me a great slug. We clinked glasses. My man emptied his, and I put mine down without bringing it to my lips, because I had never drunk pure wine, and its odor disgusted me. I admitted this to my mentor, who cried in a loud voice, "Waiter! . . . bring a lemonade for this boy who never drinks wine! . . . " And great bursts of laughter echoed throughout the entire room! . . . I was totally mortified, but could not

[3] A tall, cylindrical military cap.

force myself to taste that wine and dared not order water: I thus ate without drinking!

Learning the military life is very hard at any time. It was especially difficult at the time of which I speak. I had several bad moments to get through. Most intolerable was the obligation of sleeping with another hussar, for the regulation assigned only one bed to every two soldiers. Only noncommissioned officers were allowed to sleep alone. The first night I spent in the barracks, I had just lain down when a giant, gangly hussar, who had arrived an hour after the others, approached my bed and, seeing that I was already in it, held a lamp under my nose to examine me more closely, then got undressed. Even while watching him do this, I was far from thinking that he intended to get in next to me; but I soon learned otherwise when he told me harshly, "Move over, conscript!" Then he lay down in the bed, taking up three quarters of it, and began to snore at great volume! I could not sleep, especially because of the frightful odor emitted by the big package my comrade had placed under the pillow to elevate his head. I could not understand what it could be. To find out, I slipped my hand quietly toward that object and found a leather apron, completely impregnated with rope makers' resin! . . . My amiable bed-comrade was one of the regimental boot maker's assistants! I felt such revulsion that I got up, dressed, and went to sleep in the stables on a pile of straw. The next day, I told Pertelay of my misadventure, who related it to the platoon's second lieutenant. . . . Understanding how unpleasant it was for me to sleep with a boot maker, [he] had me given a bed in the noncommissioned officers' room, which gave me great pleasure.

Although the Revolution had brought about great relaxation in the bearing of the troops, the 1st Hussars had kept its tone exactly as in the days when it had been Bercheny; consequently, except for their natural physical dissimilarities, all the cavalrymen had to resemble one another, and since the hussar regiments then wore not only a pigtail, but also long tresses on their temples and upturned mustaches, everyone who belonged to the unit was required to have mustaches, pigtail, and tresses. Since I had none of these, my mentor led me to the squadron wig maker, who gave me a false pigtail and attached tresses to my hair, which was already long since I had let it grow since enrolling. At first, these accoutrements embarrassed me; but I got used to them in a few days, and they pleased me, because I imagined that they gave me the air of an *old hussar*; but it was not the same with the mustaches: I had no more of those than a young girl, and since a hairless face would have ruined the beautiful uniformity of the squadron's ranks, Pertelay, in conformity with the custom in the Bercheny Regiment, took a pot of black wax and with his thumb drew two enormous curved mustaches which covered my upper lip and ran almost up to my eyes. And since at this time the shakos had no visors, it sometimes happened to me during reviews or when I was standing guard duty—in both situations one had to keep completely still—that the Italian sun, casting its burning rays on my face, struck the moist wax with which my mustaches had been made, and, liquefying, this wax pulled on my skin in a most disagreeable manner! Yet I still did not budge! I was a hussar! To me, there was something magical about this word; moreover, in taking up the military career, I had well understood that my first duty was to obey regulations. . . .

In performing the service of a simple hussar, my father's principal aim had been to rid me of that naive schoolboy air, which my short stay in Paris had done nothing to diminish. The result exceeded his hopes, since, living in the midst of rough-and-tumble hussars and having for mentor a sort of brute who laughed at the stupid things I did, I began to howl with the wolves and, fearing that they would make fun of my timidity, I became a real devil. I was not enough of one, however, to enter the brotherhood which, under the name of *clique*, had members in all the squadrons of the 1st Hussars.

The clique was formed of the regiment's wildest and bravest soldiers. Its members supported one another against all outsiders, especially against the enemy. . . . They identified themselves by a cut gouged out with a knife from the tin of the first button on the right side of their fur jacket and vest. The officers knew of the clique; but since its worst misdeeds were limited to skillfully plundering chickens and muttons, or playing pranks on civilians, and since they always took the lead in combat, they turned a blind eye to the clique.

I was so stupid that I burned to join this society of brawlers; I thought it would position me favorably among my comrades; but even though I frequently practiced [different kinds of sword fighting], the saber, the pistol, and the musket, even though I elbowed everybody in my way, dragged my saber, and placed my shako over my ear, the members of the clique, seeing me as a child, refused to admit me among them.

2

BENJAMIN HARRIS

Recollections

1848

Benjamin Randell Harris (1781–?) was raised in southern England in humble social circumstances. He had no formal education and was illiterate. His family were shepherds, an occupation he practiced. In 1803, the Peace of Amiens collapsed, and Britain mobilized for renewed warfare with France. Harris became a private in the 66th Foot Regiment. He was in his early twenties. He first served in England and Ireland, where he transferred to the 95th Regiment, an elite sharpshooter unit. In 1807 he accompanied his regiment to Denmark and, the following year, to Portugal. In 1808 and 1809, Harris fought in the Iberian Peninsula. In 1809 his regiment was withdrawn from Spain and landed in Holland as part of the ill-fated Walchern expedition. The British were decimated by disease, and Harris, evacuated to England in 1809 with the remnants of the expedition, spent the rest of the war in and out of hospitals. He was demobilized in 1814 and became a shoemaker. Sometime in the 1830s he met an old comrade, Captain Henry Curling, who recorded Harris's war reminiscences. The manuscript was published in 1848. It is one of the few accounts of the Napoleonic Wars by a common soldier. It is remarkable for its detailed descriptions of the hardships of battle and military life for soldiers as well as for the wives and other female camp followers who accompanied the troops.

My father was a shepherd, and I was a sheep-boy from my earliest youth. Indeed, as soon almost as I could run, I began helping my father to look after the sheep on the downs of Blandford, in Dorsetshire, where I was born.[1] Whilst I continued to tend the flocks and herds under my charge, and occasionally (in the long winter nights) to learn the art of making shoes, I grew a hardy little chap, and was one fine day in the

---

[1] Unless essential for understanding the narrative, locations will not be glossed.

Recollections of Rifleman Harris (Old 95th.) *with Anecdotes of His Officers and His Comrades,* ed. Henry Curling, Esq. (London: H. Hurst, 1848), 1–280.

year 1802, drawn as a soldier for the Army of Reserve. Thus, without troubling myself much about the change which was to take place in the hitherto quiet routine of my days, I was drafted into the 66th Regiment of Foot, bid good-bye to my shepherd companions, and was obliged to leave my father without an assistant to collect his flocks, just as he was beginning more than ever to require one; nay, indeed, I may say to want tending and looking after himself, for old age and infirmity were coming on to him; his hair was growing as white as the sleet of our downs, and his countenance becoming as furrowed as the ploughed fields around. However, as I had no choice in the matter, it was quite as well that I did not grieve over my fate.

My father tried hard to buy me off, and would have persuaded the Sergeant of the 66th that I was of no use as a soldier, from having maimed my right hand (by breaking the fore-finger when a child). The Sergeant, however, said I was just the sort of little chap he wanted, and off he went, carrying me (amongst a batch of recruits he had collected) away with him. . . .

On arriving at Winchester, we found the whole regiment there in quarters. Whilst lying at Winchester (where we remained three months), young as I was in the profession, I was picked out, amongst others, to perform a piece of duty that, for many years afterwards, remained deeply impressed upon my mind, and gave me the first impression of the stern duties of a soldier's life. A private of the 70th Regiment had deserted from that corps, and afterwards enlisted into several other regiments; indeed, I was told at the time (though I cannot answer for so great a number) that sixteen different times he had received the bounty[2] and then stolen off. Being, however, caught at last, he was brought to trial at Portsmouth, and sentenced by general court-martial to be shot.

The 66th received a route to Portsmouth, to be present on the occasion, and, as the execution would be a good hint for us young 'uns, there were four lads picked out of our corps to assist in this piece of duty, myself being one of the number chosen.

Besides these men, four soldiers from three other regiments were ordered on the firing-party, making sixteen in all. The place of execution was Portsdown Hill, near Hilsea Barracks, and the different regiments assembled must have composed a force of about fifteen thousand men, having been assembled from the Isle of Wight, from Chichester, Gosport, and other places. The sight was very imposing, and appeared to make a deep impression on all there. As for myself, I felt that I would

---

[2] A cash reward paid to new soldiers when they joined up.

have given a good round sum (had I possessed it) to have been in any situation rather than the one in which I found myself; and when I looked into the faces of my companions, I saw, by the pallor and anxiety depicted in each countenance, the reflection of my own feelings. When all was ready, we were moved to the front, and the culprit was brought out. He made a short speech to the parade, acknowledging the justice of his sentence, and that drinking and evil company had brought the punishment upon him.

He behaved himself firmly and well, and did not seem at all to flinch. After being blindfolded, he was desired to kneel down behind a coffin, which was placed on the ground, and the Drum-Major of the Hilsea depôt, giving us an expressive glance, we immediately commenced loading.

This was done in the deepest silence, and, the next moment, we were primed and ready. There was then a dreadful pause for a few moments, and the Drum-Major, again looking towards us, gave the signal before agreed upon (a flourish of his cane), and we leveled and fired. We had been previously strictly enjoined to be steady, and take good aim, and the poor fellow, pierced by several balls, fell heavily upon his back; and as he lay, with his arms pinioned to his sides, I observed that his hands waved for a few moments, like the fins of fish when in the agonies of death. The Drum-Major also observed the movement, and making another signal, four of our party immediately stepped up to the prostrate body, and placing the muzzles of their pieces to the head, fired, and put him out of his misery. The different regiments then fell back by companies, and the word being given to march past in slow time, when each company came in line with the body, the word was given to "mark time," and then "eyes left," in order that we might all observe the terrible example. . . .

Whilst in Winchester, we got a route for Ireland, and embarking at Portsmouth, crossed over and landed at Cork. There we remained nine weeks; and being a smart figure and very active, I was put into the light company of the 66th, and, together with the light corps of the other regiments, we were formed into light battalions, and sent off to Dublin. Whilst in Dublin, I one day saw a corps of the 95th Rifles, and fell so in love with their smart, dashing, and devil-may-care appearance, that nothing would serve me till I was a Rifleman myself; so, on arriving at Cashel one day, and falling in with a recruiting-party of that regiment, I volunteered into the 2nd battalion. This recruiting-party were all Irishmen, and had been sent over from England to collect (amongst others) men from the Irish Militia, and were just about to return to England. I think they were as reckless and devil-may-care a set of men as ever I beheld, either before or since.

Being joined by a Sergeant of the 92nd Highlanders, and a Highland Piper of the same regiment (also a pair of real rollicking blades), I thought we should all have gone mad together. We started on our journey, one beautiful morning, in tip-top spirits, from the Royal Oak, at Cashel; the whole lot of us (early as it was) being three sheets in the wind.[3] When we paraded before the door of the Royal Oak, the landlord and landlady of the inn, who were quite as lively, came reeling forth, with two decanters of whiskey, which they thrust into the fists of the Sergeants, making them a present of decanters and all, to carry along with them, and refresh themselves on the march. The Piper then struck up, the Sergeants flourished their decanters, and the whole route commenced a terrific yell. We then all began to dance, and danced through the town, every now and then stopping for another pull at the whiskey decanters. Thus we kept it up till we had danced, drank, shouted, and piped thirteen Irish miles, from Cashel to Clonmel. Such a day, I think, I never spent, as I enjoyed with these fellows; and on arriving at Clonmel, we were as glorious as any soldiers in all Christendom need wish to be. In about ten days after this, our Sergeants had collected together a good batch of recruits, and we started for England. Some few days before we embarked (as if we had not been bothered enough already with the unruly Paddies[4]), we were nearly pestered to death with a detachment of old Irish women, who came from different parts (on hearing of their sons having enlisted), in order to endeavour to get them away from us. Following us down to the water's edge, they hung to their offspring, and, dragging them away, sent forth such dismal howls and moans that it was quite distracting to hear them. . . .

At length we got our lads safe on board, and set sail for England.

No sooner were we out at sea, however, than our troubles began afresh with these hot-headed Paddies; for, having now nothing else to do, they got up a dreadful quarrel amongst themselves, and a religious row immediately took place, the Catholics reviling the Protestants to such a degree that a general fight ensued. The poor Protestants (being few in number) soon got the worst of it, and as fast as we made matters up among them, they broke out afresh and began the riot again.

From Pill, where we landed, we marched to Bristol, and thence to Bath. . . .

From Bath we marched to Andover, and when we came upon Salisbury Plain, our Irish friends got up a fresh row. At first they appeared

---

[3] Very drunk.
[4] Derogatory term for Irish people.

uncommonly pleased with the scene, and, dispersing over the soft carpet of the Downs, commenced a series of Irish jigs, till at length as one of the Catholics was setting to his partner (a Protestant), he gave a whoop and a leap into the air, and at the same time (as if he couldn't bear the partnership of a heretic any longer), dealt him a tremendous blow with his shillelagh,[5] and stretched him upon the sod. This was quite enough, and the bludgeons immediately began playing away at a tremendous rate. . . .

We had, I remember, four officers with us, and they did their best to pacify the pugnacious recruits. One thrust himself amongst them, but was instantly knocked down for his pains, so that he was glad enough to escape. After they had completely tired themselves, they began to slacken in their endeavours, and apparently to feel the effect of the blows they dealt each other, and at length suffered themselves to be pacified, the officers got them into Andover.

Scarcely had we been a couple of hours there, and obtained some refreshment, ere these incorrigible blackguards again commenced quarrelling, and, collecting together in the streets, created so serious a disturbance that the officers, getting together a body of constables, seized some of the most violent and succeeded in thrusting them into the town jail; upon this their companions again collected, and endeavoured to break open the prison gates.

Baffled in this attempt, they rushed through the streets knocking down every body they met. The drums now commenced beating up for a volunteer corps of the town, which, quickly mustering, drew up in the street before the jail, and immediately were ordered to load with ball.

This somewhat pacified the rioters, and our officers persuading them to listen to a promise of pardon for the past, peace was at length restored among them.

The next day we marched for Ashford, in Kent, where I joined the 95th Rifles, and about six months after my joining, four companies of the second battalion were ordered on the expedition to Denmark. We embarked at Deal, and sailing for the hostile shores, landed on a little place called, I think, Scarlet Island, somewhere between Elsineur and Copenhagen.

The expedition consisted of about 30,000 men, and at the moment of our getting on shore, the whole force set up on simultaneous and tremendous cheer, a sound I cannot describe, it seemed so inspiring. This, indeed, was the first time of my hearing the style in which our men

---

[5] A large club.

give tongue when they get near the enemy, though afterwards my ears became pretty well accustomed to such sounds. As soon as we got on shore, the Rifles were pushed forward as the advance, in chain order, through some thick woods of fir, and when we had cleared these woods and approached Copenhagen, sentries were posted on the roads and openings leading towards the town, in order to intercept all comers, and prevent all supplies. Such posts we occupied for about three days and nights, whilst the town was being fired on by our shipping. I rather think this was the first time of Congreve rockets[6] being brought into play, and as they rushed through the air in the dark, they appeared like so many fiery serpents, creating, I should think, terrible dismay among the besieged. . . .

I felt so much exhilarated that I could hardly keep back, and was checked by the Commander of the company (Capt. Leech), who called to me by name to keep my place. About this time, my front-rank man, a tall fellow named Jack Johnson, shewed a disposition as though the firing had on him an effect the reverse of what it had on many others of the company, for he seemed inclined to hang back, and once or twice turned round in my face. I was a rear-rank man, and porting my piece, in the excitement of the moment I swore that if he did not keep his ground, I would shoot him dead on the spot; so that he found it would be quite as dangerous for him to return as to go on.

I feel sorry to record the want of courage of this man, but I do so with the less pain as it gives me the opportunity of saying that during many years' arduous service, it is the only instance I remember of a British soldier endeavouring to hold back when his comrades were going forward. . . .

While in Denmark we led a tolerably active life, the Rifles being continually on the alert—order hither to-day, and countermanded the next. Occasionally, too, when wanted in a hurry, we were placed in carts, and rattled over the face of the country, in company with the dragoons of the German Legion; so that, if we had not so much fighting as afterwards in the Peninsula, we had plenty of work to keep us from idleness.

Occasionally, also, we had some pleasant adventures among the blue-eyed Danish lasses, for the Rifles were always terrible fellows in that way.

One night, I remember, a party of us had possession of a gentleman's house, in which his family were residing. The family consisted of the

---

[6] Early explosive rockets, named for their inventor.

owner of the mansion, his wife, and five very handsome daughters, besides their servants.

The first night of our occupation of the premises the party was treated with the utmost civility, and everything was set before us as if we had been their equals; for although it was not very pleasant to have a company of foreign soldiers in the house, it was doubtless thought best to do everything possible to conciliate such guests. Accordingly, on this night, a large party of the green-jackets unceremoniously sat down to tea with the family.

Five beautiful girls in a drawing-room were rather awkward companions for a set of rough and ready Riflemen, unscrupulous and bold, and I cannot say I felt easy. All went on very comfortably for some time; our fellows drank their tea very genteelly, whilst one young lady presided at the urn to serve it out, and the others sat on each side of their father and mother, chatting to us, and endeavouring to make themselves as agreeable as they could.

By and bye, however, some of our men expressed themselves dissatisfied with tea and toast, and demanded something stronger; and liquors were accordingly served to them. This was followed by more familiarity, and, the ice once broken, all respect for the host and hostess was quickly lost. I had feared this would prove the case, and on seeing several of the men commence pulling the young ladies about, kissing them, and proceeding to other acts of rudeness, I saw that matters would quickly get worse, unless I interfered. Jumping up, therefore, I endeavoured to restore order, and upbraided them with the blackguardism of their behaviour after the kindness with which we had been used.

This remonstrance had some effect; and when I added that I would immediately go in quest of an officer, and report the first man I saw ill use the ladies, I at length succeeded in extricating them from their persecutors. . . .

Soon after this the expedition returned to England, and I came with others of the Rifles, in a Danish man-of-war (the Princess Caroline), and landed at Deal, from whence we had started.

From Deal we marched to Hythe, and there we lay until the year 1808, and in that year four companies of the second battalion, to which I belonged, were ordered to Portugal. . . .

We sailed majestically out of the Cove of Cork for the hostile shore, where we arrived safely, and disembarked at Mondego Bay. . . .

Being immediately pushed forwards up the country in advance of the main body, many of us, in this hot climate, very soon began to find out the misery of the frightful load we were condemned to march and fight under, with a burning sun about our heads, and our feet sinking every step into the hot sand.

The weight I myself toiled under was tremendous, and I often wonder at the strength I possessed at this period, which enabled me to endure it; for, indeed, I am convinced that many of our infantry sank and died under the weight of their knapsacks alone. For my own part, being a handicraft, I marched under a weight sufficient to impede the free motions of a donkey; for besides my well-filled kit, there was the great-coat rolled on its top, my blanket and camp kettle, my haversack, stuffed full of leather for repairing the men's shoes, together with a hammer and other tools (the lapstone I took the liberty of flinging to the devil), ship-biscuit and beef for three days. I also carried my canteen filled with water, my hatchet and rifle, and eighty rounds of ball cartridge in my pouch; this last, except the beef and biscuit, being the best thing I owned, and which I always gave the enemy the benefit of, when opportunity offered. . . .

The next day we again advanced, and being in a state of the utmost anxiety to come up with the French, neither the heat of the burning sun, long miles, or heavy knapsacks were able to diminish our ardour. Indeed, I often look back with wonder at the light-hearted style, the jollity, and reckless indifference with which men who were destined in so short a time to fall, hurried onwards to the field of strife; seemingly without a thought of anything but the sheer love of meeting the foe and the excitement of the battle.

It was five or six days before the battle of Rolica, the army was on the march, and we were pushing on pretty fast. The whole force had slept the night before in the open fields; indeed, as far as I know (for the Rifles were always in the front at this time), they had been for many days without any covering but the sky. . . .

[In the battle] the 29th regiment received so terrible a fire, that I saw the right wing almost anihilated, and the colonel (I think his name was Lennox) lay sprawling amongst the rest. We had ourselves caught it pretty handsomely; for there was no cover for us, and we were rather too near. The living skirmishers were lying beside heaps of their own dead; but still we had held our own till the battalion regiments came up. "Fire and retire"[7] is a very good sound; but the Rifles were not over fond of such notes. We never performed that manoeuvre, except when it was made pretty plain to us that it was quite necessary; the 29th,

---

[7] "Fire and retire" is one of the bugle sounds to the skirmishers, when hard-pressed.

however, had got their fairing[8] here at this time; and the shock of that fire seemed to stagger the whole line, and make them recoil. . . .

At the time I was remarking these matters (loading and firing as I lay), another circumstance divided my attention. . . . A man near me uttered a scream of agony; and, looking from the 29th, who were on my right, to the left, whence the screech had come, I saw one of our sergeants, named Frazer, sitting in a doubled-up position, and swaying backwards and forwards, as though he had got a terrible pain in his bowels. He continued to make so much complaint, that I arose and went to him, for he was rather a crony of mine.

"Oh! Harris!" said he, as I took him in my arms, "I shall die! I shall die! The agony is so great that I cannot bear it."

It was, indeed, dreadful to look upon him; the froth came from his mouth, and the perspiration poured from his face. Thank Heaven! he was soon out of pain; and, laying him down, I returned to my place. Poor fellow! he suffered more for the short time that he was dying than any man I think I ever saw in the same circumstances. I had the curiosity to return and look at him after the battle. A musket-ball, I found, had taken him sideways, and gone through both groins.

Within about half-an-hour after this I left Sergeant Frazer, and, indeed, for the time, had as completely forgotten him, as if he had died a hundred years back. The sight of so much bloodshed around, will not suffer the mind to dwell long on any particular casualty, even though it happen to one's dearest friend. There was no time either to think, for all was action with us Rifles just at this moment; and the barrel of my piece was so hot from continual firing, that I could hardly bear to touch it, and was obliged to grasp the stock beneath the iron, as I continued to blaze away. James Ponton was another crony of mine (a gallant fellow!); he had pushed himself in front of me, and was checked by one of our officers for his rashness. "Keep back, you Ponton!" the lieutenant said to him, more than once. But Ponton was not to be restrained by anything but a bullet when in action. This time he got one; which, striking him in the thigh, I suppose hit an artery, for he died quickly. The Frenchmen's balls were flying very wickedly at that moment; and I crept up to Ponton, and took shelter by lying behind, and making a rest for my rifle of his dead body. It strikes me that I revenged his death by the assistance of his carcase. At any rate, I tried my best to hit his enemies hard. There were two small buildings in our front; and the French, having managed to get into them, annoyed us much from that quarter. A

[8] Bloodying.

small rise in the ground close before these houses also favoured them; and our men were being handled very severely in consequence. They became angry, and wouldn't stand it any longer. One of the skirmishers, jumping up, rushed forward, crying, "Over, boys!—over! over!" when instantly the whole line responded to the cry, "Over! over! over!" They ran along the grass like wildfire, and dashed at the rise, fixing their sword-bayonets as they ran. The French light bobs[9] could not stand the sight, but turned about, and fled; and, getting possession of their ground, we were soon inside the buildings. After the battle was over, I stepped across to the other house I have mentioned, in order to see what was going on there; for the one I remained in was now pretty well filled with the wounded (both French and English,) who had managed to get there for a little shelter. Two or three surgeons, also, had arrived at this house, and were busily engaged in giving their assistance to the wounded, now also here lying as thickly as in the building which I had left; but what struck me most forcibly was, that from the circumstance of some wine-butts having been left in the apartment, and their having in the engagement been perforated by bullets, and otherwise broken, the red wine had escaped most plentifully, and ran down upon the earthen floor, where the wounded were lying, so that many of them were soaked in the wine with which their blood was mingled. . . .

Soon afterwards the firing commenced, and we had advanced pretty close upon the enemy. Taking advantage of whatever cover I could find, I threw myself down behind a small bank, where I lay so secure, that, although the Frenchmen's bullets fell pretty thickly around, I was enabled to knock several over without being dislodged; in fact, I fired away every round I had in my pouch whilst lying on this spot.

At length, after a sharp contest, we forced them to give ground, and, following them up, drove them from their position in the heights, and hung upon their skirts till they made another stand, and then the game began again.

The Rifles, indeed, fought well this day, and we lost many men. They seemed in high spirits, and delighted at having driven the enemy before them. Joseph Cochan was by my side loading and firing very industriously about this period of the day. Thirsting with heat and action, he lifted his canteen to his mouth; "Here's to you, old boy," he said, as he took a pull at its contents. As he did so a bullet went through the canteen, and perforating his brain, killed him in a moment. Another man fell close to him almost immediately, struck by a ball in the thigh.

[9] Light infantry.

Indeed we caught it severely just here, and the old iron was also playing its part amongst our poor fellows very merrily. I saw a man named Symmonds struck full in the face by a round shot, and he came to the ground a headless trunk. Meanwhile, many large balls bounded along the ground amongst us so deliberately that we could occasionally evade them without difficulty. I could relate many more of the casualties I witnessed on this day, but the above will suffice. When the roll was called after the battle, the females who missed their husbands came along the front of the line to inquire of the survivors whether they knew anything about them. Amongst other names I heard that of Cochan called in a female voice, without being replied to.

The name struck me, and I observed the poor woman who had called it, as she stood sobbing before us, and apparently afraid to make further inquiries about her husband. No man had answered to his name, or had any account to give of his fate. I myself had observed him fall, as related before, whilst drinking from his canteen; but as I looked at the poor sobbing creature before me, I felt unable to tell her of his death. At length Captain Leech observed her, and called out to the company, "Does any man here know what has happened to Cochan? If so, let him speak out at once."

Upon this order I immediately related what I had seen, and told the manner of his death. After awhile Mrs. Cochan appeared anxious to seek the spot where her husband fell, and in the hope of still finding him alive, asked me to accompany her over the field. She trusted, notwithstanding what I had told her, to find him yet alive.

"Do you think you could find it?" said Captain Leech, upon being referred to.

I told him I was sure I could, as I had remarked many objects whilst looking for cover during the skirmishing.

"Go then," said the captain, "and shew the poor woman the spot, as she seems so desirous of finding the body."

I accordingly took my way over the ground we had fought upon, she following and sobbing after me, and, quickly reaching the spot where her husband's body lay, pointed it out to her.

She now soon discovered all her hopes were in vain; she embraced a stiffened corpse, and after rising and contemplating his disfigured face for some minutes, with hands clasped, and tears streaming down her cheeks she took a prayer-book from her pocket, and kneeling down, repeated the service for the dead over the body. When she had finished she appeared a good deal comforted, and I took the opportunity of beckoning to a pioneer I saw near with some other men, and together we dug a hole, and quickly buried the body. Mrs. Cochan then returned with me to the company to which her husband had been attached, and laid herself down upon the heath near us. She lay amongst some other females, who were in the same distressing circumstances with herself, with the sky for her canopy, and a turf for her pillow, for we had no tents with us. Poor woman! I pitied her much; but there was no remedy. If she had been a duchess she must have fared the same. She was a handsome woman, I remember, and the circumstance of my having seen her husband fall, accompanied her to find his body, begot a sort of intimacy between us. The company to which Cochan had belonged, bereaved as she was, was now her home, and she marched and took equal fortune with us to Vimiero. She hovered about us during that battle, and then went with us to Lisbon, where she succeeded in procuring a passage to England. Such was my first acquaintance with Mrs. Cochan. The circumstances of our intimacy were singular, and an attachment grew between us during the short time we remained together. What little attention I could pay her during the hardships of the march I did, and I also offered on the first opportunity to marry her. "She had, however, received too great a shock on the occasion of her husband's death ever to think of another soldier," she said; she therefore thanked me for my good feeling towards her, but declined my offer, and left us soon afterwards for England. . . .

Towards evening I was posted upon a rising ground, amongst a clump of tall trees. There seemed to have been a sharp skirmish here, as three Frenchmen were lying dead amongst the long grass upon the spot where I was standing. As I threw my rifle to my shoulder, and walked past them on my beat, I observed they had been plundered, and their haversacks having been torn off, some of the contents were scattered about. Among other things, a small quantity of biscuit lay at my feet.

War is a sad blunter of the feelings, I have often thought since those days. The contemplation of three ghastly bodies in this lonely spot failed then in making the slightest impression upon me. The sight had become, even in the short time I had been engaged in the trade, but too familiar. The biscuits, however, which lay in my path, I thought a blessed windfall, and, stooping, I gathered them up, scraped off the blood with which they were sprinkled with my bayonet, and ate them ravenously. . . .

Next day was devoted to the duty of burying the dead and assisting the wounded, carrying the latter off the field into a churchyard near Vimiero.

The scene in this churchyard was somewhat singular. Two long tables had been procured from some houses near, and were placed end to end amongst the graves, and upon them were laid the men whose limbs it was found necessary to amputate. Both French and English were constantly lifted on and off these tables. As soon as the operation was performed upon one lot, they were carried off, and those in waiting hoisted up: the surgeons with their sleeves turned up, and their hands and arms covered with blood, looking like butchers in the shambles. I saw as I passed at least twenty legs lying on the ground, many of them being clothed in the long black gaiters then worn by the infantry of the line. The surgeons had plenty of work on hand that day, and not having time to take off the clothes of the wounded, they merely ripped the seams and turned the cloth back, proceeding with the operation as fast as they could.

Many of the wounded came straggling into this churchyard in search of assistance, by themselves. I saw one man, faint with loss of blood, staggering along, and turned to assist him. He was severely wounded in the head, his face being completely incrusted with the blood which had flowed during the night, and had now dried. One eyeball was knocked out of the socket, and hung down upon his cheek.

Another man I observed who had been brought in, and propped against a grave-mound. He seemed very badly hurt. The men who had carried him into the churchyard, had placed his cap filled with fragments of biscuit close beside his head, and as he lay he occasionally turned his mouth towards it, got hold of a piece of biscuit, and munched it.

As I was about to leave the churchyard, Dr. Ridgeway, one of the surgeons, called me back, to assist in holding a man, he was endeavouring to operate upon.

"Come and help me with this man," he said, "or I shall be all day cutting a ball out of his shoulder."

The patient's name was Doubter, an Irishman. He disliked the doctor's efforts, and writhed and twisted so much during the operation that it was with difficulty Dr. Ridgeway could perform it. He found it necessary to cut very deep, and Doubter made a terrible outcry at every fresh incision.

"Oh, doctor dear!" he said, "it's murdering me you are! Blood an' 'ounds! I shall die!—I shall die! For the love of the Lord don't cut me all to pieces!"

Doubter was not altogether wrong; for, although he survived the operation, he died shortly afterwards from the effects of his wounds. . . .

Many trivial things which happened during the retreat to Corunna, and which on any other occasion might have entirely passed from my memory, have been, as it were, branded into my remembrance, and I recollect the most trifling incidents which occurred from day to day during that march. I remember, amongst other matters, that we were joined, if I may so term it, by a young recruit, when such an addition was anything but wished for during the disasters of the hour. One of the men's wives (who was struggling forward in the ranks with us, presenting a ghastly picture of illness, misery, and fatigue), being very large in the family-way, towards evening stepped from amongst the crowd, and lay herself down amidst the snow, a little out of the main road. Her husband remained with her; and I heard one or two hasty observations amongst our men, that they had taken possession of their last resting-place. The enemy were, indeed, not far behind at this time, the night was coming down, and their chance seemed in truth but a bad one. To remain behind the column of march in such weather was to perish, and we accordingly soon forgot all about them. To my surprise, however, I, some little time afterwards (being myself then in the rear of our party), again saw the woman. She was hurrying, with her husband, after us, and in her arms she carried the babe she had just given birth to. Her husband and herself, between them, managed to carry that infant to the end of the retreat, where we embarked. God tempers the wind, it is said, to the shorn lamb; and many years afterwards I saw that boy, a strong and healthy lad. The woman's name was M'Guire, a sturdy and hardy Irishwoman; and lucky was it for herself and babe that she was so, as that night of cold and sleet was in itself sufficient to try the constitution of most females. I lost sight of her, I recollect, on this night, when the darkness came upon us; but with the dawn, to my surprise, she was still amongst us.

The shoes and boots of our party were now mostly either destroyed or useless to us, from foul roads and long miles, and many of the men were entirely barefooted, with knapsacks and accoutrements altogether in a dilapidated state. The officers were also, for the most part, in as miserable a plight. They were pallid, way-worn, their feet bleeding, and their faces overgrown with beards of many days' growth. What a contrast did our corps display, even at this period of the retreat, to my remembrance of them on the morning their dashing appearance captivated my fancy in Ireland! Many of the poor fellows, now near sinking with fatigue, reeled as if in a state of drunkenness, and altogether I thought we looked the ghosts of our former selves; still we held on resolutely. . . .

About this period I remember another sight, which I shall not to my dying day forget; and it causes me a sore heart, even now, as I remember it. Soon after our halt beside the turnip-field the screams of a child near me caught my ear, and drew my attention to one of our women, who was endeavouring to drag along a little boy of about seven or eight years of age. The poor child was apparently completely exhausted, and his legs failing under him. The mother had occasionally, up to this time, been assisted by some of the men, taking it in turn to help the little fellow on; but now all further appeal was vain. No man had more strength than was necessary for the support of his own carcass, and the mother could no longer raise the child in her arms, as her reeling pace too plainly shewed. Still, however, she continued to drag the child along with her. It was a pitiable sight, and wonderful to behold the efforts the poor woman made to keep the boy amongst us. At last the little fellow had not even strength to cry, but, with mouth wide open, stumbled onwards, until both sank down to rise no more. The poor woman herself had, for some time, looked a moving corpse; and when the shades of evening came down, they were far behind amongst the dead or dying in the road. This was not the only scene of the sort I had witnessed amongst the women and children during that retreat. Poor creatures! They must have bitterly regretted not having accepted the offer which was made to them to embark at Lisbon for England, instead of accompanying their husbands into Spain. The women, however, I have often observed, are most persevering in such cases, and are not to be persuaded that their presence is often a source of anxiety to the corps they belong to. . . .

After hobbling some distance down the lane, to my great joy I espied a small hut or cabin, with a little garden in its front; I therefore opened the small door of the hovel, and was about to enter when I considered that most likely I should be immediately knocked on the head by the inmates if I did so. The rain, I remember, was coming down in torrents at this time, and, reflecting that to remain outside was but to die, I resolved at all events to try my luck within. I had not much strength left; but I resolved to sell myself as dearly as I could. I therefore brought up my rifle, and stepped across the threshold. As soon as I had done so, I observed an old woman seated beside a small fire upon the hearth. She turned her head as I entered, and immediately upon seeing a strange soldier, she arose, and filled the hovel with her screams. As I drew back within the doorway, an elderly man, followed by two, who were apparently his sons, rushed from a room in the interior. They immediately approached me; but I brought up my rifle again, and cocked it, bidding them keep their distance.

After I had thus brought them to a parley, I got together what little Spanish I was master of, and begged for shelter for the night and a morsel of food, at the same time lifting my feet and displaying them a mass of bleeding sores. It was not, however, till they had held a tolerably long conversation among themselves that they consented to afford me shelter; and then only upon the condition that I left by daylight on the following morning. I accepted the conditions with joy. Had they refused me, I should indeed not have been here to tell the tale. Knowing the treachery of the Spanish character, I however refused to relinquish possession of my rifle, and my right hand was ready in an instant to unsheath my bayonet, as they sat and stared at me whilst I devoured the food they offered.

All they gave me was some coarse black bread, and a pitcher of sour wine. It was, however, acceptable to a half-famished man; and I felt greatly revived by it. Whilst I supped, the old hag, who sat close beside the hearth, stirred up the embers, that they might have a better view of their guest, and the party meanwhile overwhelmed me with questions, which I could neither comprehend nor had strength to answer. I soon made signs to them that I was unable to maintain the conversation, and begged of them, as well as I could, to shew me some place where I might lay my wearied limbs till dawn.

Notwithstanding the weariness which pervaded my whole body, I was unable for some time to sleep except by fitful snatches, such was the fear I entertained of having my throat cut by the savage-looking wretches still seated before the fire. Besides which, the place they had permitted me to crawl into was more like an oven than anything else, and being merely a sort of berth scooped out of the wall, was so filled with fleas and other vermin, that I was stung and tormented most miserably all night long.

Bad as they had been, however, I felt somewhat restored by my lodging and supper, and with the dawn I crawled out of my lair, left the hut, retraced my steps along the lane, and once more emerged upon the high-road, where I found my companion, the sergeant, dead, and lying where I had left him the night before.

I now made the rest of my way along the road in the direction in which I had last seen our army retreating the night before. A solitary individual, I seemed left behind amongst those who had perished. It was still raining, I remember, on this morning, and the very dead looked comfortless in their last sleep, as I passed them occasionally lying on the line of march. . . .

After progressing some miles, I came up with a cluster of poor devils who were still alive, but apparently, both men and women, unable to proceed. They were sitting huddled together in the road, their heads drooping forward, and apparently patiently awaiting their end.

Soon after passing these unfortunates, I overtook a party who were being urged forward under charge of an officer of the 42nd Highlanders.

He was pushing them along pretty much as a drover would keep together a tired flock of sheep. They presented a curious example of a retreating force. Many of them had thrown away their weapons, and were linked together arm-in-arm, in order to support each other, like a party of drunkards. They were, I saw, composed of various regiments; many were bare-headed, and without shoes; and some with their heads tied up in old rags and fragments of handkerchiefs.

I marched in company with this party for some time, but as I felt after my night's lodging and refreshment in better condition I ventured to push forwards, in the hope of rejoining the main body, and which I once more came up with in the street of a village.

On falling in with the Rifles, I again found Brooks, who was surprised at seeing me still alive; and we both entered a house, and begged for something to drink. I remember that I had a shirt upon my back at this time, which I had purchased of a drummer of the Ninth regiment before the commencement of the retreat. It was the only good one I had; I stripped, with the assistance of Brooks, and took it off, and exchanged it with a Spanish woman for a loaf of bread, which Brooks, myself, and two other men, shared amongst us.

Slowly and dejectedly crawled our army along. Their spirit of endurance was now considerably worn out, and judging from my own sensations, I felt confident that if the sea was much further from us, we must be content to come to a halt at last without gaining it. I felt something like the approach of death as I proceeded—a sort of horror, mixed up with my sense of illness—a reeling I have never experienced before or since. Still I held on; but with all my efforts, the main body again left me behind. Had the enemy's cavalry come up at this time I think they would have had little else to do but ride us down without striking a blow.

It is, however, indeed astonishing how man clings to life. I am certain that had I lain down at this period, I should have found my last billet on the spot I sank upon. Suddenly I heard a shout in front, which was prolonged in a sort of hubbub. Even the stragglers whom I saw dotting the road in front of me seemed to have caught at something like hope; and as the poor fellows now reached the top of a hill we were ascending, I heard an occasional exclamation of joy—the first note of the sort I had heard for many days. When I reached the top of the hill the thing spoke for itself. There, far away in our front, the English shipping lay in sight. . . .

After the disastrous retreat to Corunna, the Rifles were reduced to a sickly skeleton, if I may so term it. Out of perhaps nine hundred of as active and fine fellows as ever held a weapon in the field of an enemy's country, we paraded some three hundred weak and crest-fallen invalids. . . .

After awhile, some of the strongest and smartest of our men were picked out to go on the recruiting service, and gather men from the militia regiments to fill up our ranks. I myself started off with Lieutenant Pratt, Sergeant-Major Adams, and William Brotherwood. . . .

I was a shoemaker in the corps, and had twenty pounds in my pocket which I had saved up. With this money, I hired a gig,[10] and the Sergeant-Major and myself cut a very smart figure. The only difficulty was, that neither of us knew how to drive very well, consequently we overturned the gig on the first day, before we got half way on our journey, and the shafts being broken we were obliged to leave it behind us in a small village, midway between Hythe and Rye, and take to our legs, as was more soldierly and seemly. We reached Rye the same night, and I recollect that I succeeded in getting the first recruit there, a strong, able-bodied chimney-sweep, named John Lee. This fellow (whose appearance I was struck with as he sat in the taproom of the "Red Lion" on that night, together with a little boy as black and sooty as himself) offered to enlist the moment I entered the room, and I took him at his word, and immediately called for the Sergeant-Major for approval.

"There's nothing against my being a soldier," said the sweep, "but my black face; I'm strong, active, and healthy, and able to lick the best man in this room."

"Hang your black face," said the Sergeant-Major; "the Rifles can't be too dark: you're a strong rascal, and if you mean it, we'll take you to the doctor to-morrow and make a [general] of you the next day." So we had the sweep that night into a large tub of water, scoured him outside, and filled him with punch inside, and made a Rifleman of him.

The Sergeant-Major, however, on this night, suspected from his countenance, what afterwards turned out to be the case, that Lee was rather a slippery fellow, and might repent. So, after filling him drunk, he said to me—"Harris, you have caught this bird, and you must keep him fast. You must both sleep to-night handcuffed together in the same bed, or he will escape us;" which I actually did. . . .

After rejoining Sergeant-Major Adams at Rye, we started off for Hastings in Sussex, and on our way we heard of the East Kent Militia at Lydd; so we stopped there about an hour to display ourselves before them, and try if we could coax a few of them into the Rifles. We strutted up and down before their ranks arm-in-arm, and made no small sensation amongst them. When on the recruiting service in those days, men were accustomed to make as gallant a show as they could, and accordingly we had both smartened ourselves up a trifle. The Sergeant-Major

[10] A two-wheeled carriage.

was quite a beau, in his way; he had a sling belt to his sword like a field-officer, a tremendous green feather in his cap, a flaring sash, his whistle and powder-flask displayed, an officer's pelisse[11] over one shoulder, and a double allowance of ribbons in his cap; whilst I myself was also as smart as I dared appear, with my rifle slung at my shoulder.

In this guise we made as much of ourselves as if we had both been Generals, and, as I said, created quite a sensation, the militia-men cheering us as we passed up and down, till they were called to order by the officers.

The permission to volunteer was not then given to the East Kent, although it came out a few days afterwards, and we persuaded many men, during the hour we figured before them, that the Rifles were the only boys fit for them to join.

After looking up the East Kent, we reached Hastings that same night, where we found that the volunteering of the Leicester Militia (who were quartered there) had commenced, and that one hundred and twenty-five men and two officers had given their names to the 7th Fusileers, and these, Adams and I determined to make change their minds in our favor if we could. . . .

We worked hard in this business. I may say that for three days and nights we kept up the dance and the drunken riot. Every volunteer got ten guineas bounty, which, except the two kept back for necessaries, they spent in every sort of excess, till all was gone. Then came the reaction. The drooping spirits, the grief at parting with old comrades, sweethearts, and wives, for the uncertain fate of war. And then came on the jeers of the old soldier; the laughter of Adams and myself, and comrades, and our attempts to give a fillip to their spirits as we marched them off from the friends they were never to look upon again; and as we termed it, "shove them on to glory"—a glory they were not long in achieving, as out of the hundred and fifty of the Leicestershire, which we enlisted in Hastings, scarce one man, I should say, who served, but could have shewn at the year's end some token of the fields he had fought in; very many found a grave, and some returned to Hythe with the loss of their limbs. . . .

At Deal, the Rifles embarked in the Superb, a seventy-four,[12] and a terrible outcry there was amongst the women upon the beach on the embarkation; for the ill consequences of having too many women amongst us had been so apparent in our former campaign and retreat, that the allowance of wives was considerably curtailed on this occasion,

---

[11] A fur-lined jacket.
[12] A warship carrying seventy-four cannons.

and the distraction of the poor creatures at parting with their husbands was quite heart-rending; some of them clinging to the men so resolutely, that the officers were obliged to give orders to have them separated by force. In fact, even after we were in the boats and fairly pushed off, the screaming and howling of their farewells rang in our ears far out at sea. . . .

A fair wind soon carried us off Flushing, where one part of the expedition disembarked; the other made for South Beveland[13] among which latter I myself was. . . .

The appearance of the country (such as it was) was extremely pleasant, and for a few days, the men enjoyed themselves much. But at the expiration of (I think) less time than a week, an awful visitation came suddenly upon us. The first I observed of it was one day as I sat in my billet, when I beheld whole parties of our Riflemen in the street shaking with a sort of ague, to such a degree that they could hardly walk; strong and fine young men who had been but a short time in the service seemed suddenly reduced in strength to infants, unable to stand upright—so great a shaking had seized upon their whole bodies from head to heel. The company I belonged to was quartered in a barn, and I quickly perceived that hardly a man there had stomach for the bread that was served out to him, or even to taste his grog,[14] although each man had an allowance of half-a-pint of gin per day. In fact I should say that, about three weeks from the day we landed, I and two others were the only individuals who could stand upon our legs. They lay groaning in rows in the barn, amongst the heaps of lumpy black bread they were unable to eat.

This awful spectacle considerably alarmed the officers, who were also many of them attacked. The naval doctors came on shore to assist the regimental surgeons, who, indeed, had more upon their hands than they could manage; Dr. Ridgeway of the Rifles, and his assistant, having nearly five hundred patients prostrate at the same moment. . . .

Under these circumstances, which considerably confounded the doctors, orders were issued (since all hopes of getting the men upon their legs seemed gone) to embark them as fast as possible, which was accordingly done with some little difficulty. The poor fellows made every effort to get on board; those who were a trifle better than others crawled to the boats; many supported each other; and many were carried helpless as infants. . . .

---

[13] Harris is describing his participation in the disease-ridden expedition to Walchern Island (Holland).
[14] An alcoholic drink.

The hospital at Hythe being filled with the sick, the barracks became a hospital, and as deaths ensued, and thinned the wards, the men were continually removed, making a progress from barrack to hospital, and from hospital to the grave. The ward of the hospital in which I myself was, accommodated eleven men, and I saw, from my bed in the corner where I lay, this ward refilled ten times, the former patients being all carried out to the grave. I had been gradually removed as the men died, until I was driven up into a corner of the ward, where I lay, and had plenty of leisure to observe my comrades in misfortune, and witness their end. Some I beheld die quietly, and others were seized in various ways. Many got out of bed in shivering delirium, and died upon the floor in the night-time. . . .

The medical men made every effort to trace the immediate cause of this mortality amongst us; and almost all the men were examined after death; but it was of no avail, as nothing could arrest the progress of the malady after it had reached a certain height. The doctor, I heard, generally attributed the deaths, in most cases, to enlargement of the spleen, as almost all were swollen and diseased in that part. I myself was dreadfully enlarged in the side, and for many years afterwards carried "an extra paunch."

As soon as the prospect began to brighten, and the men to recover a little, we managed to muster outside the hospital, some three hundred of us parading there morning and evening, for the benefit of fresh air; and medicine was served out to us as we stood enranked, the hospital orderlies passing along the files, and giving each man his dose from large jugs which they carried.

As we got better, an order arrived to furnish two companies of the second battalion, and two companies of the third battalion, of Rifles, for Spain, as they were much wanted there. Accordingly an inspection took place, and two hundred men were picked out, all of whom were most anxious to go. I myself was rejected at that time, as unfit, which I much regretted. However, on making application, after a few days, I was accepted, principally on the recommendation of Lieutenant Cochrane, who much wished for me; and I, in consequence, once more started for foreign service.

From Hythe to Portsmouth, where we were to embark, was eight days' march; but the very first day found out some of the Walcheren lads. I myself was assisted that night to my billet, the ague having again seized me, and on the third day waggons were put in requisition to get us along the road. As we proceeded, some of those men who had relapsed died by the way, and were buried in different places we passed through.

At Chichester, I recollect, a man was taken out of the waggon in which I myself lay, who had died beside me; and at that place he was buried.

At Portsmouth I remained one night, billeted with my fellow-travelers at the Dolphin. Here I was visited by an uncle who resided in the town; and who was much shocked at seeing me so much reduced, concluding it was impossible I could survive many days. Such was the sad state we were again reduced to. The next morning spring-waggons were procured for us, and we were sent back to Hilsea barracks for the benefit of medical advice; and I took a farewell of my uncle, expecting never to see him again. Such, however, was not to be the case, as, out of the thirty-nine Riflemen who went to Hilsea hospital, I alone survived. . . .

After this, being the only Rifleman left at Hilsea, Lieutenant Bardell made application to the General for leave for me to go into Dorsetshire to see my friends, which was granted; but the doctor shook his head, doubting I should ever be able to endure the journey. In about a week, however, I considered myself fit to undertake it; and, accordingly, a non-commissioned officer of one of the line regiments put me into a Salisbury coach. A lady and gentleman were my fellow passengers inside, and we started about four o'clock. They seemed not much to relish the look of a sick soldier in such close quarters; and, indeed, we had hardly cleared the town of Gosport before I gave them a dreadful fright. In short, I was attacked all at once with one of my periodical ague-fits, and shook to so desperate a degree that they were both horror-struck, and almost inclined to keep me company in my trembling. The lady thought that both herself and husband were lost, and would certainly catch the complaint; expressing herself as most unhappy in having begun her journey on that day. These fits generally lasted an hour and a quarter, and then came on a burning fever, during which I called for water at every place where the coach stopped. In fact, coachman, guard, and passengers, outside and in, by no means liked it, and expected every minute that I should die in the coach.

"Here's a nice go," said the coachman, as he stopped at a place called Whitchurch, "catch me ever taking up a sick soldier again if I can help it. This here poor devil's going to make a die of it in my coach."

It seemed, indeed, as if I had personally offended the burly coachman, for he made an oration at every place he stopped at, and sent all the helpers and idlers to look at me, as I sat in his coach, till at last I was obliged to beg of him not to do so. . . .

At length, early in the morning, the coach stopped at a village one mile from my father's residence, which was on the estate of the present Marquis of Anglesey. I had left my father's cottage quite a boy, and although I knew the landlord of the little inn where the coach stopped, and several other persons I saw there, none recognised me; so I made myself known as well as I could, for I was terribly exhausted, and the landlord immediately got four men to carry me home.

My father was much moved at beholding me return in so miserable a plight, as were also my stepmother and my brother. I remained with them eight months, six of which I lay in a hopeless state in bed, certificates being sent every month to Hythe, stating my inability to move; and during which time Captain Hart sent four letters to the commanding officer, desiring I might be drafted out, if possible, to Spain, as, being a handicraft, I was much wanted there. . . .

At the end of the eighth month (being once more somewhat recovered, and able to crawl about, with the aid of a stick, a few yards from our cottage door), as my mother-in-law had once or twice expressed herself burthened by this long illness, I resolved to attempt to return to my regiment. I was therefore transported in a cart to the King's Arms Inn, at Dorchester, my body being swollen up hard as a barrel, and my limbs covered with ulcers. Here the surgeons of the 9th and 11th Dragoons made an examination of me, and ordered me into Dorchester hospital, where I remained seven weeks; and here my case completely puzzled the faculty.

At length Dr. Burroughs, on making his rounds, caught sight of me as I sat on my bed, dressed in my green uniform.

"Hallo! Rifleman," he said, "how came you here?"

Being told, he looked very sharply at me, and seemed to consider.

"Walcheren," he inquired, "eh?"

"Yes, sir," I said, "and it has not done with me yet."

"Strip, my man," he said, "and lie on your back. What have you done for him?" he asked sharply of the doctor.

The doctor told him.

"Then try with him mercury,[15] sir," he said, "both externally and internally."

After saying which, in a rapid manner, he turned as quickly, and proceeded in his rounds amongst the rest of the patients.

I was now salivated most desperately, after which I got a little better, and resolved, at all hazards, to try and rejoin my regiment, for I was utterly tired of the hospital life I had altogether so long led. "For Heaven's sake," I said, "let me go and die with my own regiment!"

---

[15] Then considered a curative, now known to be toxic.

With some little difficulty I got leave to go, and once again started, at my own expense, for Hythe, in Kent, by the coach. . . .

When I made my appearance in the barrack-square at Hythe, I was like one risen from the dead; for I had been so long missing from amongst the few I knew there, that I was almost forgotten. A hardy Scot, named McPherson, was one of the first who recognised me.

"Eh, my certie," he said, "here's Harris come back. Why I thought, man, ye was gane amangst the lave o' them, but the devil will na kill ye, I think!"

The day after my arrival I was once more in hospital, and here I remained under Dr. Scott for twenty-eight weeks. Such was the Walcheren fever, and to this day I sometimes feel the remains of it in damp weather. From Hythe I was sent, amongst other invalids, to Chelsea. Sixty of us marched together on this occasion. Many had lost their limbs, which, from wounds as well as disease, had been amputated; and altogether we did not make a very formidable appearance, being frequently obliged to be halted in the road to repair our strength, when the whole turn-out would be seen sitting or sprawling at full length by the way-side.

This march took us ten days to accomplish, and when we halted at Pimlico, we were pretty well done up. We were billeted in the different public houses in Chelsea. With others, I lodged at the Three Crowns, close beside the Bun House.

I remember we paraded in the Five Fields, then an open space, but now covered with elegant mansions, and become a part of London. Three thousand invalids mustered here every morning—a motley group, presenting a true picture of the toils of war. There were the lame, the halt, and the blind, the sick, and the sorry, all in a lump. With those who had lost their limbs, there was not much trouble, as they became pensioners; but others were, some of them, closely examined from day to day as to their eligibility for service. Amongst others I was examined by Dr. Lephan.

"What age are you, Rifleman?" he said.

"Thirty-two, sir," I replied.

"What trade have you been of?" he inquired.

"A shoemaker," I replied.

"Where have you been?" he said.

"In Denmark, Spain, Portugal, and Walcheren," I said, "in which latter place I met the worst enemy of all."

"Never mind that," he said, "you'll do yet; and we will send you to a Veteran Battalion." . . .

I remained in the Veterans only four months, as, at the expiration of that time, Napoleon was sent to Elba. We were then marched to Chelsea, to be disbanded, where we met thousands of soldiers lining the streets, and lounging about before the different public-houses, with every description of wound and casualty incident to modern warfare. There hobbled the maimed light-infantry man, the heavy dragoon, the hussar, the artillery-man, the fusileer, and specimens from every regiment in the service. The Irishman, shouting and brandishing his crutch; the English soldier, reeling with drink; and the Scot, with grave and melancholy visage, sitting on the steps of the public-house amongst the crowd, listening to the skirl of his comrades' pipes, and thinking of the blue hills of his native land. . . .

In about a week's time I was discharged, and received a pension of sixpence per day. . . . Before, however, my pension became due, I was again called upon to attend, together with others, in consequence of the escape of Bonaparte from Elba; but I was then in so miserable a plight with the remains of the fever and ague, which still attacked me every other day, that I did not answer the call, whereby I lost my pension.

3

LOUIS-GABRIEL MONTIGNY

Account of a Canteen Woman

1833

Of the different types of women who accompanied the troops, none were more colorful than the cantinières *of the French armies. Providing drink and tobacco to the soldiers, sharing their hardships (and sometimes their beds), these women were a fixture of the military community. They were typically of modest social background, poorly educated, and often illiterate, and no* cantinière *is known to have kept a diary or written a memoir of her experiences. Fortunately, some French officers left accounts of these women. The document excerpted here was written by Louis-Gabriel*

Louis-Gabriel Montigny, *Souvenirs annecdotiques d'un officier de la Grande Armée* (Paris, 1833), 322–35. Thomas Cardoza kindly provided this source.

Montigny (?–1846), an infantry officer in the Grand Army. After the fall of the empire, Montigny left the service and became a writer. His description of Marie Tête-de-Bois (Wooden-Head) is the most detailed literary depiction of a cantinière *known to exist. Marie was a famous* cantinière *of the Napoleonic Wars, known for her force of character, vulgarity, courage, and ugliness. Her renown—and possibly Montigny's fascination with her—was due to the sharp contrast between her behavior and bearing and the ideals of proper feminine comportment prevalent at the time.*

Marie Wooden-Head was a *cantinière*, not a fancy one with horse and cart, who changes her underwear and dress and goes about seated comfortably on her vehicle, sheltered from wind and rain. No. Marie went on foot. . . . Like our infantry, she wore gaiters and straw-soled shoes. Marie smelled like spirits, garlic, tobacco—every possible regimental odor. . . .

When Marie spoke, to make sure that the words you heard really came from a woman's mouth, you had to fix your eyes on her coarse wool, pleated skirt. If you didn't, you'd think you were hearing a vulgar dragoon.

Marie's face resembled one of those old wig makers' heads that we still see sometimes at the village barbers', with a little nose and enormous lips. My word, she was repulsive.

That is how she got her name, Marie Wooden-Head.

To get Marie to think of cleanliness, which she almost always neglected, the customer had to remark, when she was filling his glass during a halt or in bivouac,[1] . . . that the only glass she ever used in her business still bore visible traces [of her last customer]. Then and only then, Marie would plunge her four fingers and thumb into the glass and rotate them several times to clean and dry it.

When death took her (we will soon see where and how), Marie was fifty years old and had served in seventeen campaigns.

She never claimed to have ever been pretty. She did not recall ever having possessed the qualities of a virtuous and innocent maiden. When it came to virtue, she was a total skeptic; she believed in fruits, but not in flowers. That was her firm philosophy.

When asked where she had had the misfortune to lose what nobody in the regiment could remember her ever possessing [her virtue], Marie

---

[1] Military encampment.

shrugged her shoulders and insulted whoever teased her about it by calling him a conscript, even if he were the senior sapper[2] of the unit. A singular adventure was told about Marie.

At Marengo, while in bivouac the night after the battle (she was almost nine months pregnant), she felt sudden pains while she was blowing hard on a fire, probably made with green wood. Her efforts to ignite this recalcitrant fire were extraordinary. Completely absorbed in this business, Marie did not notice a certain change taking place. A passing grenadier, hearing a curious sound, cried: "Marie, you've dropped something."

And, in effect, the size of the army had just grown by one little boy, whose birth interested the whole regiment.

Marie was born at the Invalides, long before the Revolution. Her blind father had a job there. One suspects that it was because of his blindness that she prematurely learned many things that women hardly learn in adulthood.

Her first military experience was with the Army of Sambre-et-Meuse. Tired of spoon-feeding her old father, as she said in her energetic language, she put herself under the protection of a drummer. . . .

Marie wasn't ungrateful. She had an excellent heart, and, as long as her father was alive, she gave him her savings; but at the Invalides, he was too close. Feeling herself born for independence, she left her mother, a washerwoman, the responsibility of taking care of him.

Marie led rather than followed our soldiers in the diverse lands where we carried the glory of our arms. She was always at the head of her adoptive regiment. On the day of battle, her place was at the most perilous post. Marie didn't believe in danger any more than she did in virtue. A Prussian or English sword would disabuse her at Waterloo.

At least twenty times she saw the personnel turn over in the light infantry regiment where *she served,* for Marie knew how to shoot. . . .

Marie utterly despised those of her peers who, in the short intervals of peace that Napoleon left Europe, respected themselves so little that they exercised the profession of her mother (washerwoman). She always said that she would feel degraded if she touched a soldiers' shirt without a soldier inside.

Marie had only one husband; she acquired him at Verona, during the 1805 campaign. That happy mortal, who soon found that his wife was right not to believe in the existence of the jewel [her virginity] so prized by Joan of Arc, was a simple grenadier and wanted no other distinction. . . . Passionately in love with the merchandise his spouse

---

[2] An infantryman specializing in combat engineering.

sold, he was her best customer and liked nothing better than to get drunk when Marie let him. Such was the empire she exercised over this worthy man that, although fierce with his comrades and fearless before the Austrians, he was as gentle as an angel with Marie. When he married her, she did not change her name; on the contrary, he took that of his wife. He was called Mister Marie in all seriousness.

The result of this tender, but unofficial, union was the brave little boy of the Marengo bivouac . . . who soon became a drummer. . . .

At fifteen, he received a rifle of honor; at twenty, a second lieutenant's commission for bravery in combat; and from then on . . . when her business was not going well, he shared his pay with his mother and refilled her little barrel of spirits when she was out of money.

One day Mister Marie made the mistake of getting killed; it was at Montmirail[3] in 1814. Marie had already lost her father and old mother many years before. And destiny was about to deal her an even more terrible blow. Her son fell before the walls of Paris the same year: A cannonball cut the unfortunate in half.

Marie was devastated. Informed of the frightful loss while distributing spirits to our betrayed warriors on the heights of Montmartre, she went to the spot where her son had received his death blow, searched for him, found the pieces, and loaded them on her shoulders, intending to carry them to the closest church for burial.

On the way, she was shot in her behind, immobilizing her. Luckily, some soldiers saw her and transported her, with her relic, to a nearby ambulance.

She healed.

Since then, Marie, who was not haughty, showed whoever would look, and without even being asked, the scar the gunshot had left.

France was restored, and Marie ruined, by the peace. Deprived of resources, she had to overcome her aversion for the profession of washerwoman; but, so as not to lose her old clientele, she established herself near one of the capital's barracks.

The emperor returned from Elba. Marie sold her clothes' irons, took up her old keg again, and left on foot for Lille, where there was a general of the Old Guard[4] who counted among his bravest exploits the courage he had once shown in forgetting himself for several instants with the Wooden-Head.

---

[3] A battle in Napoleon's campaign to defend France.
[4] Part of Napoleon's elite Imperial Guard.

She got a *cantinière*'s patent and was attached to the Guard, where she received a welcome worthy of her.

Marie recovered the freshness of her youth; she was triumphant and bore her little tricolor keg with noble pride.

However fortune was about to betray her!

At Fleurus,[5] at the height of the fighting, she was knocked over and trampled by a squadron of English dragoons fleeing from our hussars. . . .

She had herself bandaged and washed; she showed her wounded posterior to all the Old Guard, and on the morning of the 18th found herself on the Waterloo battlefield.

From the outset, she had a presentiment of our defeat, and even said it to several of our brave soldiers, but in a whisper so as not to frighten the weaker ones.

In the afternoon, feeling that there would soon be no more spirits to distribute to the unfortunates who were being betrayed, she tried to see the emperor and, when she had enjoyed this pleasure, thought only of getting herself killed.

Around 7:30 p.m., Marie was in the middle of one of the squares of the Guard, distributing liquor for free and consoling the wounded, too numerous to carry off.

At 8:00 p.m., when French voices began to cry out "Every man for himself!" Marie, determined to not survive such shame, summoned death; death came.

A sword, slashing at her from the side, cut through her keg and her body.

She fell, crying "Long live France!"

Five minutes later, while dragging herself toward a dead grenadier whom she wanted to use for a pillow, a stray shot passed through the legs of three ranks of soldiers and struck her face, disfiguring her hideously.

She cried "Long live the emperor!"

The mortally wounded grenadier she had wanted to use [as a pillow] and whom she had believed dead painfully raised himself and said: "Marie, you aren't pretty like that. . . ."

Marie answered him, trying to smile: "Maybe; but I am proud of being a girl, wife, mother, and trooper's widow!"

And then she died.

---

[5] A minor battle that preceded Waterloo.

4

French Intelligence Report on British India
1807

*The European colonial powers during the Napoleonic Wars employed
locally recruited troops to defend and maintain order in their global
possessions. To retain the loyalty of these troops, European commanders
needed to understand and respect their deeply held religious and cultural
practices. Nowhere was this challenge greater than for the British in
India, a vast subcontinent marked by great religious and ethnic diversity.
Britain's Indian troops, the sepoys, were recruited from both Hindus
and Muslims, as well as from widely differing social castes. Reconcil-
ing differences between the sepoys themselves, as well as between Indian
values and European military norms, was often difficult. Sometimes the
British failed, with spectacularly bloody results. The following document
is a French intelligence report describing a major mutiny of British sepoy
troops in the southern Indian town of Vellore. Eager to expand their own
presence on the subcontinent, the French were always on the lookout for
opportunities to profit from British troubles. This report never made it
back to France, however, for the ship that was carrying it was captured
by a British warship, and the report was later deposited in the British
National Archives.*

Since July 18, 1806, the Coromandel Coast[1] has been the theater of
events so serious that they have the potential to shake the foundation of
English power here to its very core. An order, doubtless from Europe, to
force the indigenous troops to wear hats was sent to all the sepoy units.
They received it with all the indignation that a change so contrary to
their prejudices, based on their religion and customs, would naturally
produce. They consequently complained. But whether this new market for [Britain's] national industries was considered too advantageous
to give up or for some other reason, this order was maintained. Each

---

[1] Of southeastern India, the scene of heavy fighting between the Indians and British
in the 1790s (the Mysore War). Britain had taken over the last independent Indian states
of the region in 1801, only five years before the events described here.

British National Archives, ADM 1/3977.

commander was directed to make his respective unit adopt the new headwear. They generally employed rigorous methods. The unfortunate sepoys were to be worn down by continual drilling until they accepted the fatal hats. They were so exasperated that they unanimously resolved to kill their persecutors rather than give up their turbans, because this would have assimilated them to the most vile caste of India. . . .

Consequently, on the night of August 9th [1806] the regiment in garrison at Vellore took up arms and went to the European barracks, massacred everyone unable to flee, and then fanned out across the city where these bloodthirsty insurgents forced the doors of their officers' houses. They killed seventeen or eighteen, as well as many youngsters and children. They decided to defend the fort to the bitter end, which they would surely have done if these looters had not broken into the stores of strong liquor. Most of these savages drank heavily and became drunk, so that when the white cavalry units (who had been warned by the city's major, who had managed to escape the carnage) arrived the following morning [from the nearby British possession of Arcot], more than two-thirds of the rebels were incapable of defending the place, even though they had already loaded their cannons. The gates of the fort were broken down by cannonfire, and the cavalry sabered all the individuals it found there. The camp of the blacks[2] was set on fire. The women and children of these unfortunates were burned alive. . . .

Trichinopoly[3] and generally all the cities and military bases with indigenous units were threatened with the same scenes as had occurred at Vellore. They were seizing the depots and arsenals, when special envoys ended the general alarm of the country by assuring the black troops that the order to wear hats had been revoked. But it is said that an explosion occurred at Hyderabad[4] and that more than 2,000 individuals, white and black, perished in this bloody fight. Consternation is general among the [British] inhabitants about what happened in the interior, although they are not fully aware of the facts because of the government's efforts to hide them. The government certainly believed itself in danger, because half of the crews of the vessels at Madras[5] were sent as reinforcements to the garrison. The firing mechanisms of the sepoys' muskets were removed, and the regiment that was at

---

[2] At this time, both the French and British sometimes referred to Indians as "blacks."
[3] A city in southeastern India.
[4] A city in south-central India.
[5] A port city north of Vellore.

Colombo[6] was ordered to march to the coast as quickly as possible with loaded weapons.

Since these events, several Indian princes desirous of throwing off the [British] yoke that has weighed on them for so long have carried out intensive military recruiting. All the units in the south of the peninsula are determined to turn their arms against their oppressors, and if it can be guaranteed that the French will appear on their coasts within three or four months, they would soon raise the standard of a general revolt. Altogether, they would number more than 30,000 natives determined to fight. In addition, there would be the diverse English sepoy units, whose numbers cannot be accurately estimated because of their continual movements on the coast. It is nonetheless certain that, for this sort of affair, we can count on an almost complete reunion [of disgruntled Indians]—above all, in the present situation, where the confidence of the subordinates in their leaders has been entirely destroyed, and where the [British] yoke weighs more heavily than ever on the peasants, who have just been placed at the mercy of tax farmers[7] for all commodities they desire or need: such as salt, tobacco, betel nut, opium, etc. Because of this, the unfortunate inhabitants now pay four times more than previously. It would thus not be unreasonable to count on . . . this general discontent.

Letters from Bengal[8] say that Holkar[9] is encamped on the banks of the Narbuda River with a large army and that the English are worried that there may soon be a rupture with this prince. They cannot hide the fact that never before have the Indian powers had more favorable circumstances to get their revenge, having no doubt that they will learn of the uprising that took place and the discontent agitating the entire country. . . . Tax farmers have been attacked by the natives and forced to flee; tobacco and betel nut warehouses have been pillaged. . . . Prisoners on a chain gang tried to break their bonds, but since the European troops, whom the circumstances had summoned from Colombo, had disembarked there, the escape attempt was thwarted by their unexpected arrival. Some guards were killed, as well as a large number of prisoners.

---

[6] Capital city of Ceylon (present-day Sri Lanka), then a British-held island south of India.

[7] Tax collectors.

[8] A region in northeastern India, at the time one of the centers of British power in the subcontinent.

[9] Independent ruler of the state of Indore, in central India.

5

Correspondence of William Lee, U.S. Consul in Bordeaux

1806–1809

William Lee (1772–1840) was born a British subject in Halifax, Nova Scotia. At some point during the American Revolution, his father shifted loyalties to the new country of the United States and moved to Massachusetts. His son William, author of the letters transcribed below, became a merchant in Boston in 1790. Four years later he married Susan Palfrey, daughter of the former paymaster of Washington's Continental Army. Their first child, Susan Palfrey Lee, was born in 1795. The next year Lee went to Europe, where he remained, conducting business, until 1798. In 1801 the new president, Thomas Jefferson, appointed him U.S. consul to Bordeaux, France's principal Atlantic port. Lee moved to France with his family and remained there until 1816, when he gave up his post and returned to the United States. As consul in the main port through which American merchants traded with France, Lee occupied an excellent vantage point from which to survey the effects of the Napoleonic Wars on maritime commerce. Since his main duty was to uphold American commercial interests, he routinely had to intervene on behalf of captains and merchants charged with violating both the French Continental System and the British counterblockade. The following selection of his letters — to his wife, to Secretary of State (and future president) James Madison, and to his daughter — illustrate the impact of the conflict on American trade, as well as on Americans living in wartime France.

Bordeaux, Dec. 9, 1806

To Mrs. Susan Palfrey Lee in Paris

Your letter of the 3rd has reached me, my dear S., but this day. I hope you did not entrust it to anyone to put in the office, who may have looked into it, as it contains opinions respecting some of your new acquaintances. Your letter enclosing the bill of furniture came to me yesterday. But we must now lay aside all ideas of buying furniture, and I have stopped all the workmen on the house, who were doing anything on my account.

Library of Congress, Washington, D.C., Lee-Palfrey Family Papers.

This decree[1] of the Emperor has thrown everything into the greatest confusion, and privateers are now fitting out here to attack American commerce.

The first article declares the British Islands in a state of blockade. Therefore all vessels bound to England, or that may have cleared out for England, and a market, will be taken and brought into France, if Gen. Armstrong[2] does not procure some modification of this decree, which it is not probable he will be able to do. All letters written in English are not to be permitted to pass in the post office. Write me therefore in French, and as I cannot write French, I will get my letters to you as well as I can. All British goods coming from their colonies or manufactures are to be a good prize wherever they are found. Therefore all American vessels with British goods or produce on board will be considered a good prize, and I expect to see the river full of our ships as enemies. The Minister of Marine is charged with the execution of this decree. Therefore there can be no doubt but that it is aimed at us.

This stroke puts a final end to our commerce to this city and renders, my dear girl, our situation peculiarly uncertain. I hope it will not be distressing. We shall get no news from America; for the moment a vessel arrives, her letters will be taken by the boarding officers, and those in English will not be permitted to circulate.

See all you can of Paris, and let me know when your quarter for the children is up, as I expect I shall be obliged to send for you or come for you; for in times like these we had better be together, for who knows now what will happen? Our ministers in England it is said, have made a treaty with that infernal nation. If it be a favorable one, our Government will have their hands full. One party will be for declaring in favor of France, another in favor of England; and if France captures many of our vessels, they may possibly adhere to England, in which case we should all be taken up here and put in prison or sent to Verdun.[3] We should have less favor shown to us than Englishmen receive, and that nation would be exasperated against us. The friendship you and I have shown to the individuals of this nation both in America and here would avail us nothing. My attachment to France would be a curse to me were I, in case of such an unfortunate event, to return to America, and it would be worth nothing to me here, particularly at Bordeaux, where you know I am not generally liked by the merchants, because I never would consent to do dishonorable things to gratify their views.

[1] The Berlin Decree.
[2] U.S. ambassador to France.
[3] A fortress town in eastern France.

The crisis is really alarming. I have written Gen'l Armstrong on the subject, and wish he would write me on the business, but I presume he has too much to do. . . . Husband all your money! Had I foreseen all this, I should not have expended 1,000 francs or thereabouts on this house. And as it is, I do not intend to take a lease of it for the present, until I see how the storm breaks.

Bordeaux, Dec. 10, 1807

To Secretary of State James Madison at Washington
Sir, I have just received intelligence from Mr. Lanne, my agent at Bayonne, that the brig *Hypsa and James* of Salem bound to this port has arrived there after having been visited by the British squadron at the mouth of this river, who made the following endorsement on her papers: "Warned from entering any port in France and all her dependencies, Portugal, Spain, Italian and Mediterranean ports, and the colonies of Spain and Portugal." . . .

It appears by this that the blockade is to take immediate effect, which much alarms us here for the fate of the sixteen vessels that left this last week for the United States. The measure is considered as very hostile to the United States, and it is believed the English intend carrying in as much American property as they can capture under the persuasion that they will be able to make better terms by this means with us. Under this impression I have advised all the American masters now in port to remain here, which, however, they do not incline to listen to.

We have had two arrivals at Rochelle,[4] one of them, the brig *Elias*, Capt. Dandelot, in attempting to come round here, has been captured by the English. The other, a three-master schooner from Baltimore, has been refused a pilot at Rochelle under the suspicion of her having been in England. The consignee, Mr. Andrews, has gone on to Rochelle and will I hope be able to procure a pilot or an entry. I mention these circumstances to show you that this Government appears determined not to admit any vessel to an entry that may have touched in England.

Paris, Nov. 26, 1809

To Susan Palfrey Lee at Bordeaux
My dear daughter, I intended when I set out to have given you an account of my journey [from Bordeaux to Paris]; but we were so continually on the move, and so few incidents occurred that would entertain you, that I postponed writing you until I should have seen something of Paris. I

---

[4] A French Atlantic port north of Bordeaux.

have been here more than a fortnight, and strange to tell, I have seen nothing except crowded midnight halls and full tables. . . .

The first evening we left Bordeaux, we stopped at Carbon Blanc,[5] where we were arrested by two gendarmes[6] for English prisoners, who would not suffer us to leave our room to go in search of our passports, which we had left in our carriage. The brusque and [rude] manner in which this arrest was conducted was so extremely improper, even had we been Englishmen, that I flew into one of my violent fits and treated the gendarmes with such contempt that [the mayor] and his [assistant] were called in, who recognized me and adjusted the affair. How ridiculous are some men apt to appear when armed with a little brief authority.

6

Popular Images of Napoleonic Warfare
Nineteenth Century

Military scenes were of great interest to Europeans during and after the Napoleonic Wars. In France, a number of firms sought to satisfy popular demand for military scenes by mass-producing affordable engravings treating subjects ranging from famous battle scenes to depictions of camp life. These images were distributed widely and even reached the most remote villages, thanks to the peddlers who typically sold them. Six of these engravings, produced in Epinal, France, the center of this industry, are presented here.

Governments were also interested in military images, although in a more overtly propagandistic way. By trying to influence what the engravings portrayed, either indirectly or by commissioning certain scenes, they sought to justify their engagement in the Napoleonic Wars and, if possible, cast the conflict in terms capable of eliciting popular commitment to the struggle. Even after the end of the wars in 1815, military engravings remained both popular and politicized. Together with this book's cover illustration — Goya's famous depiction of the French military repression of the Madrid uprising of May 2, 1808 — the following selection of images reveals a range of attitudes, both official and unofficial, toward military life from the celebratory to the horrific.

---

[5] A village a day's journey from Bordeaux.
[6] French military police.

Figure 1 (page 67) *Appel de Contingent Communal* (Calling Up the Communal Contingent) This popular engraving depicts young men responding to the annual draft call. The conscripts' physical appearance, posture, and facial expressions reveal their social status as well as their feelings about military service.
Bibliothèque nationale de France OA 21 (13) FOL.

Figure 2 (page 68) *Distribution de la Viande au Camp, etc.* (Distribution of Meat at Camp, etc.) This engraving is one in a series showing a variety of military scenes and the many roles soldiers performed — some of which brought them into conflict with civilians. The upper row of images depicts the butchering of fresh meat, its distribution, and its preparation by the soldiers themselves. The middle row shows two soldiers dueling, with a woman (presumably attached to one of them) looking on and weeping. The bottom row portrays soldiers running from a cottage, carrying food and livestock they have plundered. The angry peasant occupants chase them with flail and pitchfork.
Bibliothèque nationale de France LI 10 PET FOL.

Figure 3 (page 69) *Tableau de la Guerre* (War Painting) Another popular engraving from the same series as Figure 2, this one depicts further military scenes and acts of violence against civilians. The upper row focuses on various aspects of combat. The middle row shows three apparently unconnected military events: a soldier stealing from a mother and daughter, a sentry on duty, and a soldier killing a cavalryman with his sword. The bottom row features three more unconnected scenes from military life: a cavalryman pursuing an enemy horseman (equipped with a bow, so probably one of Russia's tribal soldiers), two soldiers looting the body of a slain enemy, and two more soldiers carrying off a young woman, presumably to rape her.
Bibliothèque nationale de France LI 10 PET FOL.

Figure 4 (page 70) *Siège de Sarragosse* (The Siege of Saragossa) This widely distributed engraving depicts the street fighting that ensued when the French army stormed the besieged Spanish city of Saragossa in 1808. Note the prominence of priests and nonuniformed combatants among the besieged. This illustrates the difficulty of distinguishing soldiers from civilians in the Spanish conflict, as well as in guerrilla warfare more generally.
Bibliothèque nationale de France LI 59 (1) FOL.

Figure 5 (page 71) *Passage de la Bérésina* (The Crossing of the Beresina) The chaotic French retreat across the Beresina River in 1812 is the focus of this engraving. Note the weariness and dejection of the retreating French troops, who seem to have lost all semblance of military organization. Also note the great flocks of carrion birds that followed the French army, feeding on fallen men and horses.
Bibliothèque nationale de France LI 59 (1) FOL.

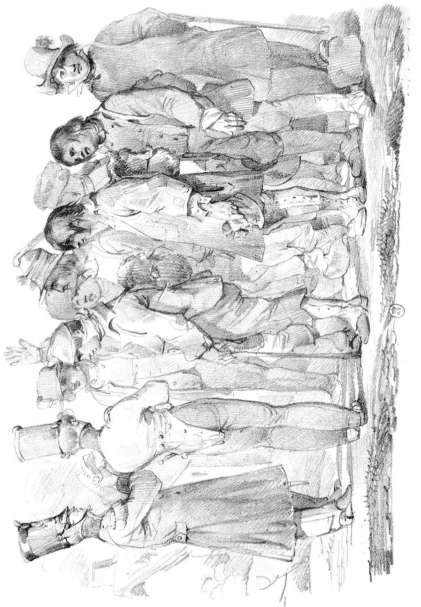

Figure 1.

67

DISTRIBUTION DE LA VIANDE AU CAMP, etc.

N.º 60

Figure 2.

TABLEAU DE LA GUERRE.

N.° 64

Figure 3.

SIÈGE DE SARRAGOSSE.

Figure 4.

70

PASSAGE DE LA BÉRÉSINA.

Figure 5.

Figure 6. *15 Août* (August 15) In this popular engraving, an elderly Napoleonic veteran is shown at home with his grandchildren on August 15, the date of the annual festival held during the Second Empire to honor Napoleon I. This image is intended to glorify the memory of military service under Napoleon I in order to reflect glory and legitimacy on the empire of his nephew, Napoleon III.

Bibliothèque nationale de France OA 21 (9) FOL.

7

GIOVANNI PATRIZI

Memoirs

c. 1817

The Marchese Giovanni Patrizi-Naro-Montoro (1775–1818) came from a prominent family of the Roman nobility. He married a German princess, Cunigunda von der Lausitz, with whom he had three sons in the 1790s. No supporter of Napoleon, he nonetheless did not openly resist French occupation and annexation of his city. However, in 1811 Napoleon tried to force the leading families of Rome to enroll their sons in French military schools and allow them to serve as officers in the imperial armies—in effect, using military service to bind the regional elites of his empire to his regime. Patrizi was horrified at turning over his sons to what he considered an ungodly regime, and he stood up in opposition. Refusing to back down, he was ultimately imprisoned in France by Napoleon. The following excerpt from his memoirs, which were written for his family and intimate friends and were only published a century after his death, describes his innermost feelings upon learning that his sons had been ordered to report to military school in France.

I can declare from my own experience that only a father, a Christian father, can conceive of what I felt when, on August 7, 1811, I received the ominous news that a large number of the sons of our Roman nobility had been summoned by an imperial decree to be educated in French military schools. I pitied the fate of the children no less than that of their parents, and I was chilled with the fear that I should all too soon be added to the number, overtaken by the same misfortune. From day to day I expected to receive the fatal announcement, but I never ceased to offer fervent prayers to Almighty God and the most Blessed Virgin that I might become childless rather than renounce my sacred right to give my sons a Christian education.

We are always ready to believe in what we desire; when a few days had passed without bringing the dreaded announcement there sprang

The Patrizi Memoirs: A Roman Family under Napoleon, 1796–1815, trans. Mrs. Hugh Fraser (New York: Brentano's, 1915), 68–74.

up in my heart the hope that, by a singular favour of Heaven, my sons were not included in the dreadful decree. And, as day followed day, this hope naturally became stronger, and I began to sleep more tranquilly.

On the twenty-ninth of August, a note from the Prefecture was brought to our house, addressed to the Marchese Patrizi. It was, of course, intended for my father; but, as at that time his health was not good, and I had taken over the management of domestic affairs to relieve him, I felt authorised to open the missive. I learnt that the Prefect, or rather his deputy (he being away on leave) desired to speak with the Marchese that very morning, and for this purpose requested him to call upon him at the hour he named. I imagined that the business had to do with agricultural matters, the extirpation of the locusts, or something of the kind, matters for the discussion of which we had, till then, sent one of our stewards. Having no desire to visit [the Prefecture] personally, I decided to follow precedent, and sent on the note to the person who had hitherto represented the family on these occasions. But I was informed, in reply to my message, that this person was very ill — as indeed was the case, for he died three weeks later.

Feeling the strongest repulsion myself to setting foot in the offices of the Prefecture, yet not wishing to appear uncivil, I wrote to that Magistrate to say that the Marchese Patrizi, being indisposed, could not do as he was requested, but would attend to the business, whatever it might be, in his own house, if someone could be sent to him there.

I had dismissed the trifling matter from my mind, when, on the afternoon of the same day, I happened to be with a friend, who asked me if anything new had taken place in regard to my sons.

"Nothing, Heaven be praised!" I replied. He congratulated me on this, and then went on to say that, during the forenoon, a great number of parents had been summoned to the Prefecture, and there informed of the Decree by which one or more of their children were ordered to military schools in France.

Great God! Only Thou knowest the pang that went through my heart at my friend's words — for now I understood the object of the intimation received that morning. I turned pale, a deadly chill came over me, and I left my friend abruptly and staggered trembling along the streets without knowing where I was going. The thought of returning home and beholding my children again filled me with dread; I sought for some ray of solace in my trouble, and found none. Nay, Religion itself, to which Christians turn for consolation in the heaviest sorrows, served only, as it were, to increase my distress. I already saw my children handed over to irreligious teachers, deprived of all means of preserving the seeds of piety implanted in their tender hearts, seduced by pernicious discourses, by wicked examples—already vacillating in their faith, corrupted in their lives, changed in a short time from innocent lambs into ravening wolves! I hoped, it is true, that the fatherly Providence of the Almighty would renew in their favour the miracle of the Furnace of Babylon; but at the same time I recognised that I could not reasonably hope for such a prodigy unless I were obliged to give up my little ones by irresistibly superior force.

These miserable reflections remained with me all through that evening, through the sleepless night which followed it, and all the next very sad day. I only spoke to a few friends of the burden which was oppressing me, and was careful not to breathe a word of it to my parents or my wife. I did not wish them to share my affliction a moment sooner than should be necessary. But, at the same time, it was beyond my powers of deception to conceal altogether the anxiety which was wringing my heart, and as in such circumstances imagination is apt to be active, I fancied, in looking at my dear ones, who were sad and silent because of my own unexplained depression, that they had heard of the Decree and were doing their best, through pure pity, to keep me in ignorance of it!

When the next day dawned—the thirty-first of August, for ever memorable as the most unfortunate of my whole life—my father sent for me very early to come to his apartment. I hastened thither and found the good old man, his face profoundly sad, his voice trembling and half inaudible as he told me what I had feared was true. "Son," he said, "in order to spare you a troubled night I would not impart to you, last evening, the distressing news which you can, alas!, too easily divine, and which was brought for you yesterday afternoon in these papers."

So speaking, he handed me a letter. My hand shook as I took it. It contained the brevets[1] by which my sons Xavier and Philip, under the imperial decree, were named as pupils at the Prytanée de la Flèche, a military school about two days' journey from Paris. The middle of September was the time set for their departure. A note from the deputy who was acting during the Prefect's absence was enclosed with the brevets, and in it the official congratulated me—ah, what an insult!—on the honour conferred upon me by the Emperor.

---

[1] Official documents.

8

JAKOB WALTER

Memoirs

c. 1820–1840

---

*Jakob Walter (1788–1864) was from the Duchy of Württemberg, a Ger-
man state allied with Napoleonic France. After primary schooling, Walter
apprenticed as a stonemason and was working in this trade in 1806,
when he was drafted into Württemberg's army for the war against Prussia.
Too late for the battles of Jena and Auerstadt, he participated in mopping-
up operations before being demobilized in 1807. He returned home and
resumed work until 1809, when he was recalled to service for the war
against Austria. Again, he missed the major battles (Aspern-Essling and
Wagram) and returned safely home in 1810. In 1812 he was mobilized
again, this time for the invasion of Russia. There, he experienced the full
intensity of Napoleonic warfare, complete with pitched battles, horrible
wounds, exhaustion, and famine. He survived the retreat from Moscow,
broken in health, and was demobilized in 1813. He resumed his civilian
career, married, and had a family. Sometime between 1820 and 1840
he wrote an account of his wartime experiences. He confided the manuscript to one of his sons, who emigrated to the United States and settled in
Kansas, in 1856. The manuscript was rediscovered in the 1930s. Walter's
memoir is the only known account by a common soldier of Napoleon's
invasion of Russia. More than officers' memoirs, it suggests what soldiers
involved in that campaign really thought and experienced and includes
vivid details about more than battles—recounting the impact of harsh
weather, disease, and the foraging for food that contributed to soldiers'
survival in total warfare.*

The march continued from Frankfurt to Poland . . . where German was
no longer spoken, and the manners and culture were unfamiliar. It was

---

*A German Conscript with Napoleon: Jakob Walter's Recollections of the Campaigns of
1806–1807, 1809, and 1812–1813, According to a Manuscript Found at Lecompton, Kansas,* ed. Otto Springer, with historical collaboration by Frank E. Melvin, *Bulletin of the
University of Kansas—Humanistic Studies,* vol. VI, no. 3 (Lawrence: University of Kansas
Department of Journalism Press, 1938), 9–135.

May. The air swarmed so thickly with May bugs that it was hard to keep your eyes open in the evening. There were so many bugs that they darkened the air, and everyone was kept busy shaking them from face and hair. Here everybody had to find and cook his own food, although foraging was forbidden. However, everyone was still strong, and courage still burned in every soldier. But each day want and hunger increased, and the regiment had to requisition and slaughter livestock so the men could have some meat with the occasional potatoes and grits they found. Bread was scarce; there was nothing to buy. . . .

On Corpus Christi Day[1] we entered Thorn,[2] on the north bank of the Vistula River, a city where I had been in 1807. Here, for the first time, we saw all the corps streaming together. The gates were jammed, and the regiments had to wind through the streets in a great throng. Nonetheless, we obtained quarters. However, we had to prepare our own food from rationed meat and bread. The meat came from salted ice pits; it was rumored that it dated from 1807. This was believable since the meat was bluish-black and as pungent as herring. It was already soft enough to eat, but we boiled it several times to extract the salt. . . .

I attended mass in the great city church, where I heard what was, for me, a very odd sermon, because it was in Polish and I could not understand it. I also climbed the high, broad tower, with more than 100 steps, and saw the eight bells. The largest bell's clapper was taller than I. . . .

Orders now routed us from Thorn to Mariapol. . . . The roads were sandy, our clothes dusty. We passed through a village called Löwenstein, where we saw a strange sight: we counted about 30 stork nests; almost all the storks nested in tall willows and went around the swamps in flocks like the geese at home. . . . Then we came to a little town called Kulvary, which lay on flat land in a barren region. Here we made a noon halt. There was nothing to eat. Since our need was great, this little town, although already plundered, was searched again. Soldiers scurried after food and water, and took the inhabitants' hidden provisions, even though it was Polish land and, thus, friendly. The townfolk complained to our Crown Prince; and so orders were given to shoot the first soldier to leave camp. I returned just in time. Our Crown Prince was so determined that he rode before us with a pistol and brandished it at the breasts of some soldiers. . . .

Hardship increased daily, there was no hope of bread. My colonel spoke to us once, saying there would be no more bread until we crossed

---

[1] A Roman Catholic holiday.

[2] Locations will not be glossed unless essential for understanding the narrative.

the enemy border. The most we still got was a little lean beef. Hunger made us dig in the fields for sprouting potatoes, which were very sweet and almost inedible. We also heard that several men had already shot themselves because of hardship; an officer had cut his throat on that very same day. Finally we reached the Niemen River, the Russian border, at the town of Poniemon. Everyone was happy to see the Russians and the frontier at last. We camped at the foot of a hill, this side of the river, and lightened our knapsacks as much as possible. I searched through my clothing and threw away vests, unnecessary cleaning articles, trousers, etc. We stayed there until pontoons were brought up and bridges built across the water. We assumed the Russians would wait on the far bank and attack, but nothing happened. Bonaparte bombarded the Russian-held heights with a few cannon and sent his cavalry across. The Russians withdrew after a short clash.

On June 25 the army crossed. We believed that, once in Russia, we could easily forage, but this was not so. Poniemon was already stripped, as were all the surrounding villages. Here and there a hog ran around until clubbed, sabered, and bayoneted; often still alive, it would be cut and torn apart. Several times I cut off something, but had to chew and eat it raw, since my hunger could not wait for a chance to boil the meat. The worst torture was marching, because the closed ranks forced us to go in columns; heat and dust flared up into our eyes as if from smoking coal heaps. The hardship was doubled by continual halting whenever we came to a swamp or narrow road. We often had to stand for half an hour; then as much time was spent catching up and sweating along without water or food.

The march proceeded day and night. . . . Cold rain fell for several days. It was all the more disagreeable because nothing dried. Bodily warmth was all that kept us from freezing to death. I had on only one pair of blue linen trousers, which I had bought at Thorn, since I had thrown away my underwear because of the previous heat. I was wet for two days and nights; not a spot on my body was dry. But I did not fall behind, although I could not see the way at night and slipped in the clay mud. Soldiers fell around me so frequently that most were completely covered with mud. Some remained lying behind.

During the third night, we halted in a field that had been trampled into a swamp. We were ordered to camp and build fires, since neither village nor forest could be seen and the rain did not let up. You can imagine our half-numbed condition. What could we do? Nothing but stack our muskets in pyramids and keep moving in order not to freeze. Finally an estate was found off to one side, and all the soldiers immediately flocked to build shelters. We had to muster all our strength to pull out poles and straw. With some help, I built a little shelter, but my strength did not last long enough to collect firewood. I lay in it, hungry and wet. However, my comrades, who came in and lay down on me, provided a warm cover.

At dawn, I hurried back to the manor. A cellar full of brandy had been discovered. I dragged myself into the cellar and filled my canteen. I returned to the shelter with it and drank without even bread. By noon I noticed that half the men had stayed back and several had drowned in the swamp. The brandy helped, but many a man drank himself to death because it numbed him and he froze from the cold and wet. My drummer, Schäfer, met such an end.

In the evening, when beef was distributed, we managed to start a fire; the meat and broth soon warmed our stomachs. Then the march continued toward the little town of Maliaduy, where we made a two-day halt, and the sick were taken to the hospital. In this bivouac, we got some meat; but since most men could no longer digest it, diarrhea seized many, and they had to be abandoned. In this camp I washed my shirt and trousers. It happened to be good weather. To get water for drinking and cooking, holes were dug into the swamps, three feet deep, in which water collected. The water was very warm, however, and was reddish-brown with millions of little red worms so that it had to be sucked through linen. . . .

The men grew weaker every day and the companies grew smaller. We marched day and night. One man after another lay down half-dead upon the ground. Most died a few hours later. Several suddenly fell to the ground dead. The chief cause was thirst, for in most districts there was no potable water, so the men had to drink from ditches full of dead horses and men. I often marched away from the columns for several hours in search of water, but rarely found any and had to go thirsty. All the towns were completely stripped and half-burned.

We finally arrived at Polozk, a big city across the Dvina River. We left camp to look for food. There were eight of us, and we came to a very distant village. We searched all the houses. There were no peasants left. Later I realized how heedless I had been, since we each ran alone into a different house, broke open everything, searched all the floors, and still found nothing. Finally, when we assembled to leave, I reinspected a little hut somewhat removed from the village. Around it from top to bottom were heaped bundles of hemp and waste-flax, which I tore down. As I worked my way to the ground, I discovered sacks of flour. I joyfully called my comrades to come help with the booty. . . .

The question of carrying and dividing the grain arose. I recalled seeing a horse at one of the houses. We immediately went to find it. We found two instead of one, but unfortunately they were both colts, and one was useless. We took the largest, placed two sacks on it, and started out very slowly. While we were marching, the Russians saw us from afar with this booty. At the same moment we saw a band of peasants in the depression, about 50. They charged us. We had no choice but to shoot at them. I, however, led the horse, and a second man held the sacks while the rest took turns firing, making the peasants disperse so as not to be hit so easily. They could not take the sacks from us.

We hurried toward the bivouac, but on the way came to a deep stream with only a round tree trunk lying across it. The question arose of how to get the horse and sacks across. I said, "I will carry the sacks across, and we will throw the horse into the water." I managed to cross the narrow bridge on foot without using handrails, a feat which might have cost me my life, since the river was quite deep. Then the horse was thrown in and driven across with stones, the sacks were reloaded, and we finally marched into bivouac. What joy! Whatever could not be used was distributed. Then dough was made, and little balls molded by hand and baked, or rather roasted, in the fire. This food lasted me a week, and I thanked God for the lucky gift which had remained buried under the flax leavings until I came.

We then marched on in a more easterly direction. . . .

We were lucky and found a village where everything still seemed intact. To protect our small group, we posted rearguards and agreed that they should fire warning shots in case of Russian attack. Upon entering the village, a man, probably sent as an interpreter from the mayor to discover what we wanted, immediately approached us. We told him we needed provisions for the army—if given voluntarily, no force would be used. He reported it to the village, but the answer was negative; so, working in pairs, we had to search the houses. I joined forces with a comrade, but found only milk and cabbage.

There was a wooden hut on a farm. It was locked, and the peasants would not open it. When we broke down the door, a pregnant woman charged us as if mad and tried to throw us out, but we pushed her back gently. We got some flour, eggs, and fat. When our findings were gathered together later, our booty was considerable. I tell this to show the ways of the Russians. If they had voluntarily revealed their storage places, their furniture would have remained unspoiled, for it was necessary to remove the floors and beams to find anything. Under one floor, which had large beams lying side by side, we found pots of sausages stuffed into casings four to five feet long and filled with pieces of bacon and meat an inch thick. Although the sausages already reeked, they were rapidly devoured. There were also hidden pots of cheese lumps. . . .

In another partly plundered village we found nothing in the houses. So, driven by hunger, we dug in the ground. We removed a large pile of wood which had probably just been put there. We removed this, dug, and found a covered plank roof. There was an opening under this, 10 to 12 feet deep. Inside were honey jars and wheat covered with straw. When we had all this, we opened the jars and saw a solid, white material resembling hard wax. It was so hard that it was difficult to cut off a piece with a saber; but when put on the fire, it melted into clear honey. I had honey to eat for a week, but no bread. I ate the wheat raw, wild swamp herbs, and garden roots. . . .

After this raiding excursion we rejoined the corps in bivouac; and on August 16 advanced on Smolensk. My company had only 25 healthy men. . . .

On the morning of August 17, all regiments were ordered to advance in columns against the Russians. Every regiment came under fire. The troops repeatedly attacked, but, outnumbered, were forced back each time, since their heavy artillery on the heights could hit everything. Finally by night we had gained a foothold on the heights above the city, and the battle ended. During it all, hunger vanished from my mind. At night, however, I ate from my little bit of honey and raw supplies without being able to cook. The thought of the coming day alternated with fitful sleep, and I dreamed of the many dead men and horses as a world of spirits before the last judgment. Since I did not suffer the misfortune of being wounded, I thought: "God, you have allowed me to live till now. I thank you and offer up my sufferings to you and pray to you at the same time to take me further into your protection."

I had this and several other pious meditations with God and contemplated my destiny. Although it was not quiet all night and though combat might have started again at any moment, none of my miseries was so hard and depressing as the thought of my brothers, sisters, and friends. This thought was my greatest pain, which I sought to repress with this hope: "With God everything is possible; so I will depend upon His further help." . . .

At daybreak we marched against the city. We crossed the river below the city. The northern suburbs were stormed, set on fire, and burned. My company's doctor, Stauble, had his arm shot off while crossing the stream and later died. I could no longer attend to my comrades and therefore did not know how they perished or were lost. Everyone fired and struck at the enemy in wild fury. No one could tell if he was in front, in the middle, or behind the center of the army.

Finally, with cannon balls raining from the city, we stormed it. With the help of heavy cannon, most of the supporting piers on the high old city wall, on which the Russians were defending themselves from the inside, were partially destroyed. We broke through the gates, pressed from all sides against the city, and put the enemy to flight. On entering the city, we went toward the cloisters and churches. I hurried into the great church which stood to the right in the city on a hill facing the valley. I did not meet any of the enemy within, however, only priests praying. They wore long black cowls, ragged pants, and old slippers. The church was large and round inside. It had many holy images and altars, like ours. The only difference was that there was no holy water. The church had five towers, one on each corner and one in the middle of the roof. On each tower were triple iron crosses, and from each cross went intervening chains from one tower to another. It was beautiful. . . .

We returned at night to our former bivouac. Here wounded men were gathered to be operated on in a brick kiln on the heights above the city. Many arms and legs were amputated and bandaged. It looked like a slaughterhouse. Over half the city's buildings were burned. . . .

On August 19, the entire army advanced on the Russians with all speed. Four or five hours farther up the river another battle started, but the enemy did not resist long. The march continued to Mosaik, the so-called "Holy Valley." From Smolensk to Mosaik, we saw war's horrible destruction. Roads, fields, and woods were strewn with people, horses, wagons, burned villages, and cities. . . . We saw 10 dead Russians for each of our men, although our numbers dropped considerably every day. To pass through woods, swamps, and tracks, barriers of felled trees had to be removed, and enemy wagon barricades had to be cleared. . . . The march was indescribable, unimaginable for people who have not experienced it. The incredible heat, the fog-like dust, the closed line of march in columns, and the warm putrid water from holes filled with dead people and cattle brought everyone close to death. Eye pains, fatigue, thirst, and hunger tormented everybody. God! how often I remembered the bread and beer I had enjoyed at home—and taken for granted! Now, however, I must struggle, half wild, with the dead and living. How gladly would I give up home-cooked food if I only had good bread and beer now! I would not wish for more my whole life. But these were empty, helpless thoughts. The thought of my distant brothers and sisters increased my pain! Wherever I looked, I saw soldiers with dead, half-desperate faces. Many cried out despairingly, "If only I had not been born!" Some demoralized men even cursed their parents for having brought them into the world.

These voices, however, raised my soul to God, and I often prayed, "God, you can save me; but, if it is not your will, I hope that my sins will be forgiven because of my sufferings and pains and that my soul will ascend to you." With such thoughts I went trustingly to my fate.

On September 7, every corps was deployed. The attack signal was given. Like thunderbolts the firing began against and from the enemy. The earth shook under the cannonfire, and the rain of balls crossed confusedly. Several earthworks were stormed and taken with heavy losses, but the enemy did not budge. The French Guard was ordered to follow up the attacking corps to achieve the final decision. The two armies moved more vigorously against each other, and the loud shouting and devastating gunfire were hellish. Nine earthworks were stormed, the French threatened to surround the enemy from the front. Finally the enemy gave way.

This beautiful grain region without woods and villages now resembled a cleared forest, a few gray and white trunks here and there. . . . The ground was covered with people and animals. There were groans and whines all around. A stream split the battlefield into two parts. . . . A burned wooden bridge crossed it. Because of the congestion before and during the burning, both banks were littered with dead three and four deep. The wounded who could still move hurried to the river to quench their thirst or wash their wounds. . . .

Although this terrible scene was like a kingdom of death, people had become so indifferent that they ran numbly like ghosts away from the piteous crying. We advanced and camped by a forest on a height facing Moscow, full of green trees. Here there was neither food nor water because of the elevation. The road through the fields was still covered with dead Russians. We went with somewhat higher hopes toward Moscow, but expected to clash again with the Russians. But they felt too weak and retreated through the city, setting fire to much of it, abandoning the inhabitants. Our troops came unexpectedly, something the Russians had believed impossible, because there had never been a foreign enemy who had reached and conquered the Tsar's old capital city. The merchants and townfolk could not flee fast enough to save themselves. Many valuables were abandoned. Even though the French Guard occupied the city first and seized wine, bread, etc., for their army, there was still much for us, the allies. . . .

Marching toward the city, from a hill in a forest an hour and a half away, we saw the huge city before us. Clouds of fire, red smoke, great gilded crosses of church towers glittered, shimmered, and billowed up toward us. This holy city was like the description of Jerusalem, over which our Savior wept. It even resembled the horror and devastation described in the Gospel. Closer to the city was a wide plain. Before the city ran the stream Alia, over which was a wooden bridge. As we marched, I observed all I could: broad streets, long straight avenues, tall buildings massively built of brick, church towers with burned roofs and half-melted bells, and copper roofs which had rolled from the buildings. Everything was vacant and uninhabitable. . . .

One could find and buy provisions. Each soldier was now citizen, merchant, innkeeper, and baker of Moscow. Everyone tried to dress in silks and colored fabrics. Only tailors were lacking; silks, muslins, and red Morocco leather were all abundant. There was no lack of food either. Those who found nothing could buy something; and quantities of vegetables stood in the fields. There were many beets, as round and large as bowling balls and fiery red throughout. There were masses of cabbage three and four times as large as cabbage heads we would consider large. The Muscovy district is more favored in agriculture and climate, and more civilized than the regions toward St. Petersburg and those we had crossed. It was still good weather. One could sleep warmly enough under a coat.

We had been citizens of Moscow for four weeks. . . . It was October 17. Napoleon held a review and announced our departure for October 18, early in the morning at 3 o'clock, with the warning that whoever should delay one hour would fall into enemy hands. All beer, brandy, etc., was abandoned. Everything left was ordered burned. Napoleon himself had the Kremlin undermined and blown up. The morning came, and each took his privilege of citizenship upon his shoulders and covered it with his strong woolen cape. Everybody had red Morocco leather bread bags at his side. All had an odd appearance as they set out; for they filled everything with as much sugar and the so-called Moscow tea as possible in order to withstand coming misery. . . .

The march began. . . . We moved past the city on the south. There were two bridges over the river below us, and smoke from the flames surged up behind us. On the heights past the bridge to the left of the road stood a cloister with a flour storeroom where everyone took as much as he could carry. Beyond the bridge was a cabbage patch with millions of cabbage heads: it hurt not to be able to take along even one, since I fully expected terrible famine.

From Moscow the road led south through Malo Jaroslavez toward Kaluga. In the evening the Russian Moldavian army, which had come from Turkey, met us near Jaroslavez. I was ordered on guard at general staff headquarters in the city while the army camped before it. Here the commanders' inhumanity began to grow: the remaining troops' weapons were inspected, and many whose weapons were not fairly rust-free got 12 to 20 club blows until they were near desperation. While I occupied my post, a comrade told me that he had a little keg of wine from Moscow on a nearby wagon and that since everything would be destroyed anyhow we should finish it. We drank and also let others drink, but we all wondered, "How will this turn out?"

In the morning Major von Schamberg saw me and noticed that I was still alert and spirited. He spoke, saying I should stay with him and take care of him along with his attendant. I agreed and took over a horse and his equipage. Then everyone packed up, and the enemy attacked us. The decision was soon to the Russians' advantage. We all ran in a crowded retreat toward Kaluga with the Cossacks before and beside us. The pursuing enemy army shattered all the army corps, leaving each of us without his commanding officer. Those too weak to carry weapons or knapsacks threw them away. We looked like a crowd of gypsies. . . .

We came to a second city, Borowsk. It was burning. To get through, the soldiers had to fight the fire. Camp was pitched by this city, and night fell. No sooner had we thought of resting than the Russians attacked our army and took many prisoners. Everything was chaotic, and during almost the whole night the throng had to retreat to Mosaik, running to avoid capture. Because of the heavy losses, hundreds of cannon, munition wagons, coaches, and baggage carts had to be thrown into the water. Where that was impossible, the wagons were burned. . . . The army supply officials, even the cavalry, had to relinquish their horses so that they could be hitched to the cannon. The fighting, shrieking, firing of large and small guns, hunger and thirst, and all conceivable torments increased the endless confusion. Even the lice seemed bent on taking us over, for there were thousands on both officers and privates.

At times when death was near, God sent me help. After midnight following the Russian pursuit, we pitched camp in a little village a quarter of an hour off the highway. I slept with my master and two horses in a stable that still had a roof. There I saw hanging on a cord behind a grate a smoked pig's head. As if received from the hand of God, I took it with a prayer of thanks. I, my master, and fellow servant devoured it, and we felt life return. I thought then: "If even a few reach German soil, I too might also get there with God's help." It snowed for the first time, and the snow remained. The cold came too, and many people froze to death, multiplying the number of dead. One could not go 50 paces without seeing bodies lying half or fully dead. . . .

Finally we went over the battlefield at Mosaik in the Holy Valley. Here we saw again in what numbers the dead lay. . . . Entire hollows were filled with corpses. Gun barrels lay in piles, from 15 to 20 feet in height and width. We bivouacked there for the night.

Here God again mysteriously helped me. While getting water with my canteen at night, I came to a lake where a hole had been made in the ice. It was hard to draw water because of the press of the crowd. On the way back, a ball resembling a dead sheep was lying on the ground. I picked it up and, in joyful amazement, unwrapped a rolled-up Crimean lamb fur that covered me from head to toe and had a peculiar collar which fit over my head. Looking heavenward, I prayed again to God and gave thanks for the abundant mercy I had received just when I needed it most.

I rushed to my major and had already put on the fur. He saw me and cried, "Aye, God! What have you got on?" "A fur I just found. . . . At least now I'm covered." "Oh," he said, "I'll give you my fur. It's also a good one. If we get home, then you can have it back, or I'll pay you enough for it." So I took his fur, which was also beautiful, with a green silk lining so it was reversible. The next morning everyone hurried on, no one wanted to be last.

We reached Gshadsk, which was already burning. Here again many cannon were thrown into the water and some buried. The press was so bad that my major and I lost each other. I now had the second horse to myself. We could not find each other again that day, nor for another 10 days.

In the evening I rode off from the army to search the outlying district for straw for the horse and rye for myself. I was not alone, for over a strip 10-hours wide famished soldiers sought food. When there was nothing to be found, they looked for cabbage stalks under the snow, cut off bits of their pulp, and let the core slowly thaw in their mouths. This time I had a second big piece of luck. I came to an unburned village where there were still sheaves of grain. I laid these before the horse and plucked off several heads of grain. I hulled them, put the kernels mixed with chaff into a hand grinder which had been left in a house, and, taking turns with several other soldiers, ground some flour. Then we rolled the dough into little fist-sized loaves and laid them on coals. Although the outside burned to charcoal, the inside was edible. I got at least 15 such balls. . . .

When this good night was half over, I laid four sheaves over my saddle and rode to the head of the army as usual. The next night, I again rode off the highway to make a fire. Trudging through the deep snow was too hard for my horse; so I took a peasant's sled with two slabs of bark for runners, put a sackcloth collar around the horse's neck, and tied two ropes from it to the sled. As I drove on again that night, I had to cross a 60-foot wide river, bridged by only four or five poles. I had to carry the sled over on the poles and force the horse to swim across. I carried the emptied sled across successfully, although my feet plunged knee-deep into the water because the poles sank. I brought the horse, which could swim well, since it was a Russian breed, to the sled again, and drove on. At this river I met a man named Wittenhüfer, from my native village, who was already very weak. I let him ride. He died a few days later.

I continued this sled-riding through the burned cities of Wiasma Semlevo and Dorogobusch without finding my master. Once, while I was eating some of my bread, several Frenchmen saw me. These inhuman men surrounded me under the pretext of buying bread. When the word "bread" was mentioned, they attacked me. I thought my death was near, but through extraordinary luck some Germans came along, to whom I called for help. They struck at my horse so that most of the Frenchmen drew back from me and then were entirely beaten off.

Among these Germans were two noncommissioned officers from my regiment called N. and N. After I was free, they took my bread and walked off. I now saw that they weren't really interested in saving me, but rather their hunger and my bread, were both my rescuers and robbers. Although I had already given them a loaf, they robbed me! But this, dear readers, must be judged differently than you think. There are stories in which people have murdered and eaten each other out of hunger, but this incident was far from murder. Since starvation had risen to such a degree, why couldn't such a thing happen? And besides that, hunger had already killed much of the men's humanity. Indeed, I even heard at that time that several men had been murdered for the sake of bread. I myself could look unmoved into the crying faces of the wounded, the freezing, and the burned, as I shall tell later, and think of other things.

We reached Smolensk on November 12, having retreated from Moscow for 26 days and nights without pause. . . .

At Smolensk it was raining heavily, and my sled could be pulled only with great effort. When I neared the city, the crowd grew so dense that for hours I could not join the column, for the guard and the artillery with the help of gendarmes knocked everyone out of the way, right and left. With effort I finally pressed through, holding my horse by the head. With swords cutting at me, I crossed the bridge. In front of the city gate I and my regiment, now disorganized, moved to the right toward the city wall beside the Dnieper River. We settled down here and camped for two days. It had been reported that we were to fight the enemy here and also draw bread and flour from the magazines. Neither report was true. The distress rose higher and higher, and horses were shot and eaten. My hunger was intense. Because I could not even get a piece of meat, I took my pot, stood beside a horse that was being shot, and caught the blood from its breast. I put it on the fire, let it coagulate, and ate the lumps unsalted.

While we stayed two days at Smolensk, the Russians advanced and awaited us at Minsk. Everyone fled. Cannon were thrown into the water. The hospitals were nearly all left to the enemy. It was widely rumored that the hospitals were set afire and burned with the patients. This seems more credible when one considers the treatment of captured Russians. When we defeated them, whole columns of captives were taken past us, and anyone who straggled from weakness and fell back to the rear guard was shot in the neck so that his brains spattered down beside him. Every 50 to 100 paces I saw another who had been shot with his head still smoking. All this was done to make our passage safe, so that no robber bands could be formed behind us. Very few of the captives were saved from starvation.

As the march continued, I had to abandon my sled and put my baggage on the horse, on which I often rode during the day. The cold increased, . . . and the road became as smooth as a mirror from the rain so that the horses fell down in droves and could not get up again. Since my horse was a native of the country, it had no horseshoes and could always help itself up again when it had fallen. It even had the good habit, when going downhill, of sitting on its rump, bracing its front legs forward, and sliding into the valley with me on its back. The German horses, however, had shoes which had been worn smooth and thus could not keep themselves from slipping; nor could these irons be removed, since no one had the necessary tools. . . .

After leaving Smolensk, we reached Krasnoi on November 16, amid a thousand dangers. The Russians met us, having circled around to our front. The French Guard and the forces that could still be mustered deployed along the highway and fired on the enemy as much as possible. Although the enemy had to yield, our movements drew heavy fire upon us. The greatest misery fell upon the sick, who usually had to be thrown from the wagons . . . and left to freeze among the enemies, for whoever remained lying behind had no hope of rescue.

Here I heard my master speak (rather yell) close in front of me. I called, "Major, is it you?" He glanced at me and cried for joy, "Oh, God, dear valet, is it you? Oh, I am glad to have you again. Oh, I am so happy you are still alive." I also showed my joy at this reunion, for my master still had his old German chestnut, his horse from home, and his other attendant was also with him with a second horse. He asked me if I still had some of his sugar loaf and coffee. Sadly I had to say that once when I lay down at night behind a battlement near a fire-razed village a group of Cuirassier Guards came at me and seized the sack with the sugar and coffee. I almost lost my horse. I therefore chose another place to lie down. In occupying my second spot I found straw lying about, which my horse could eat. I lay down on a soft, unfrozen patch. Before leaving I thought to see why it was so soft and warm under me. I saw a dead man whose unfrozen belly had been my good bed. "And I set out upon my journey again, Major, without meeting you." The Major then said, "That does not matter now. I am glad you are back." . . .

Our march continued. The striking, clubbing, and skirmishing was so awful that loud cries echoed all about. Cossacks swarmed on all sides. We approached Dubrovna, and the throng was so great that those on foot were usually beaten and cudgeled to the right and left of the road-way at narrow passages like marshes, rivers, and bridges. My major and I were pushed apart and lost each other again. It was impossible to recognize one another except by voice. Everyone was disguised in furs, rags, and pieces of cloth; they wore round hats and peasant caps, and many had priests' robes from the churches. It was like a world turned upside down. I had had enough of my helmet at the very beginning of the retreat. I put on a round hat, wrapped my head with silk and muslin and my feet with thick woolen cloth. I had on two vests and over my doublet a thick, large Russian coat which I had taken from a Russian in exchange for my own at Smolensk on the way into Russia. Over all this I wore my thick fur. I was so wrapped up that only my eyes had an opening. . . . From time to time, I had to chip off of it the ice that instantly formed from my breath.

At night in Dubrovna, when the enemy had stopped maneuvering, everyone settled down. Every night fires for warmth could be seen over a region four hours long and wide, making the sky look like red cloth. The burning villages alongside added to this spectacle. The shrieking, beating, and lamenting did not stop for a minute. Again and again people died, sometimes freezing to death; these were people who pressed toward the fire but were seldom permitted to get there. They died away from the fire, and very often their bodies were used as cushions so the living would not have to sit in the snow.

In every bivouac soldiers crept around at night like ghosts. Their complexion, their husky breathing, and their dull muttering were horrible. Wherever they went, they had no hope. No one allowed these shadows of death to drag themselves to the fire. Usually six, eight, or 10 of us had to cooperate to build a fire, since there was no wood except rafter pieces from burned houses, fallen trees, shattered wagons, etc., and without cooperation nothing was possible. Neither did we dare fall asleep at the fire at the same time, because no one was safe from theft and robbery.

As we neared Orscha, it was said we would get shoes and bread from a magazine and oats for the horses; but this was impossible. Despite the guards stationed around the storehouses, the doors could not be opened, since everyone hit and shoved each other to get close. I hurried there to obtain oats, but that was impossible until the guards gave way and the doors were thrown open. I climbed through a window, took several sacks of oats with help from my comrades, and brought them to the campfire. Immediately thereafter, a soldier who shared my fire came with two little loaves of bread. Everyone's heart beat eagerly, and we rushed toward the bread magazine. When we arrived, no one could enter any more, and those inside could not come out because of the press. What was to be done? Many weak soldiers lay on the floor and were trampled, screaming horribly. I made for a window again, tore out the shutter, wooden grating, and pane; and got five trampled loaves. Since Moscow, this was only my second bit of bread; I tearfully thanked God again. . . .

Between Orscha and Kochanova I rode off again alongside the army toward a burning village to warm myself a bit in the night and scrounge. No sooner had I lain down than Cossacks came and caught whomever they could. My horse had a peculiar intelligence (for, as soon as shots rang out, it ran with all its might). . . . It saved me by fleeing, and we returned to the army. Those on foot who had also made the side march were caught and plundered. Frenchmen were usually killed without pity by the Russians. Germans could expect mercy, they said, because the Russian Emperor had ordered that Germans be spared, since his Empress is from the house of Baden.

While on my side march, I saw on the ground a fine black bearskin with head and claws, which fugitives had had to abandon. With cries of "hurrah" I took it in the hope of bringing my belongings to Germany, for

I had various silver vessels from Moscow worth 300 to 400 florins. I also had silk goods, muslin, etc., which I was able to take in abundance from the stalled wagons. Nevertheless, it all came to nothing. . . . In the daily and nightly bustle that hardly let me rest or sleep even a few hours in four or five nights, my horse, which was tied to my arm by a strap, was cut off and led away unnoticed. Since I was accustomed to pulling on the strap upon waking to see if my horse was still there, I pulled and this time felt no horse. I jumped up—and now what? I thought to myself, even if I had the whole night to spend searching, only a miracle could lead me to my horse, and that was all the more uncertain if my horse was already on the march. However, I had to do something. I ran left and right, back and forth. Whenever I approached a horse, my life was endangered by whipping and beating, for one could not take enough precautions against theft and robbery: usually one of those sitting by the fire had to keep watch. I suddenly saw my horse standing before a chapel door with his strap tied to a sleeping soldier inside the doorway. Very softly I cut the strap and rode toward my fire. I dared not sleep any more, I thought, so that if my horse-lover returned I could speak with him.

That night I chanced into a comrade from B. called Sch. This was the third man from my district whom I met on the way from Smolensk to Moscow and back. An officer also had this man with him as a faithful friend. . . . Every soldier was like an officer now, since the uniforms showed no more distinction in rank and no superior could command a private. Officers were driven from the fire just like privates whenever they tried to push forward without just claim. Only mutual support still procured true friendship. This countryman, whom I had once liked so much, still had some rice from Moscow, though only a handful. Along with this, I had a little piece of meat which I cut off from near the ears on a dog's pelt with the whole head on it that lay near our fire. To flavor the water and warm our stomachs, we boiled the two together. When only half cooked, we started eating. Although the meat already stank a good deal and there was no salt, we devoured everything with gusto, feeling ourselves lucky to have gotten something warm.

Before setting off again, he said, "I had a loaf of bread for my master. You have taken it from me." This hurt my feelings in a way I will never forget. It is amazing how a totally false opinion can turn a friend into a scoundrel and change him into a shameful caricature of a human being over a bit of bread. Here I saw how low reason had sunk with us: our brains were frozen, and there was no feeling left. I swore and said, "Comrade, you are wrong. I have not seen or taken any bread. I would

rather give you bread than take it." It did no good. He stuck to his opinion, and death claimed him too.

Before reaching Borisov, we bivouacked behind a forest around
11 PM. It seemed the Russians had completely surrounded us, for cannonades thundered from all sides. We had to retreat hurriedly until
the enemy gave up from weariness. Everyone among us let loose with
slugging, hitting, and chasing, as if we were enemies. In bivouac, the
Germans always banded together and made fires in groups. . . . For
the most part, Württemberg sergeants and soldiers joined me at the
fire. Each one fried the horse meat he had cut off laboriously along the
way, amid shoving and hitting. For as soon as a horse fell and did not
get right up, crowds descended upon it from all sides and often cut at it
alive. The meat, unfortunately, was very lean, and only skin with a little
red meat could be wrested away. Everyone stuck his piece on a stick
or saber, burned off the hair, and waited until the outside was charred.
Then the piece was bitten off all around and stuck into the fire again.
One seldom had time for boiling, and not one in 20 men had a pot.

After the night meal, we all lay down, and I went to sleep. My horse
was tied to my arm as was my custom. In a bit one of my true comrades
cried, "You, look after your horse so it is not stolen." I said, "It's all
right here." I was not awakened again. My countrymen cut the strap and
snuck off. I awoke to find myself forsaken. "God," I thought, "who can
save me? What can I do? I cannot carry my possessions and my master's
any farther. I am so weak, I cannot even carry my fur, but I'll freeze to
death without it." These thoughts made me despondent, and increasing
pain wracked my body. I had to take a risk. . . . About 100 paces away
were the French Cuirassier Guards who had earlier taken my coffee
and sugar loaf while in camp. I will dare to take a horse! I crept near,
observing which men did not move and seemed asleep, cut a strap, and
made off with a very large black horse. I went to an isolated place some
distance away, then ran to get my luggage, loaded it on, and moved on
without delay. If only the owner does not spot me, I thought! Fearing
this, I later traded the horse.

Before daylight, as I rode thoughtfully along, I heard my master again,
Major von Schamberg. I called his name, at which he warmly rejoiced
and said, "Now we are together again." He told how he had managed
to keep alive until now, and I did the same. He was particularly glad
that I had cared for his luggage and regained a horse. After we reached
Borisov, we bivouacked again. We came to a lumberyard and built a fire.
When the Major warmed up a bit, his "subjects" plagued him sorely, and
he asked me to kill the ones in his shirt collar. I did, but, when I opened

it, there was raw flesh where the greedy beasts had gnawed. I had to look away in disgust and reassure him that I saw nothing, that my eyes stung so much from the smoke that I could not see. These pests, however, were on me too, thousands of them. . . .

As I paced around the courtyard, I saw about 20 cows which must have died from hunger and cold. When I tried to cut something from them with my saber, they were frozen rock-hard, and only with the greatest effort did I finally rip a belly open. Since I could cut or tear loose nothing but the entrails, I took a lot of tallow.[3] I would stick some on my saber and warm it just enough in the fire for most of it to remain unmelted, and I would eagerly eat one piece after another. What I had heard before—that eating tallow kept one awake—I found was true. For about 14 days I had tallow, which I ate only in the greatest emergency. . . .

On November 25, 1812 we reached Borisov. The march then turned toward the Beresina River, where indescribable horror awaited us. On the way I met one of my countrymen, Brenner, who had served with the Light Horse Regiment. He came toward me, drenched and half frozen, and we greeted each other. Brenner said that the night before he and his horse had been caught and plundered, but that he had fled through an unfrozen river. Now, he said, he was near death from freezing and starvation. This good, noble soldier had run into me not far from Smolensk with a little two-pound loaf of bread and asked me whether I wanted a piece, saying that this was his last supply. "Because you have nothing, I will share it with you." He had dismounted, laid the bread on the ground, and cut it in two with his saber. "Dear, good friend," I had replied, "you treat me like a brother. For as long as I live, I will not forget your good deed, but will repay you many times if we live!" . . . This second meeting, with both of us helpless and utterly miserable, broke my heart. We were separated, and death overtook him.

As we approached the Beresina River, Napoleon ordered his pack horses unharnessed, and he ate. He watched his army pass by in the most wretched condition. It is impossible to guess what he felt in his heart. His outward manner seemed indifferent and unconcerned over his soldiers' wretchedness. He may have felt only ambition and lost honor in his heart. Although the French and Allies shouted oaths and curses about his guilty person, he heard them unmoved. . . .

Afterwards, I met a man with a sack of raw bran with hardly any flour dust. I begged him relentlessly to sell me a little, pressing a silver

[3] Beef fat.

ruble into his hand. He put a few handfuls in my little cloth, although very unwillingly, after which I happily continued my journey. When my master and I neared the Beresina, we camped on a near-by hill, and by contributing wood I obtained a place at a fire. I immediately mixed some snow with my bran, balled it together into a fist-sized lump, which because of its brittleness broke into three or four pieces in the fire, and allowed it to get red-hot on the outside so as to obtain something like bread from the inside. My master and I ate it all with the greatest appetite.

After a time, from about 2 to 4 p.m., the Russians pressed closer on all sides, and the murdering and torturing seemed about to annihilate everyone. Although our remaining artillery was placed on a hill and fired at the enemy as much as possible, what chance was there of rescue? We expected that everyone would be captured, killed, or drowned. Everyone thought his final hour had come. . . . There was no hospital for the wounded; men also died of hunger, thirst, cold, and despair, uttering complaints and curses with their last breath. Our sick, almost entirely officers, who had been conveyed here in wagons, were abandoned; deathly white faces and stiff hands stretched toward us.

When the cannonade abated somewhat, my master and I rode downstream for about half an hour to a village with several unburned houses. The Württemberg general staff was there. At night, . . . I looked for something to eat with candles I had found. I found some spotted green cabbage which looked like rubbish. I placed it over a fire and cooked it for about half an hour. Suddenly cannonballs crashed into the village, and with a wild cheer the enemy sprang upon us. We escaped only because we mounted and rode away as fast as possible. I couldn't leave my pot of cabbage behind, but held it firmly in my arms on the horse. The fear that I might lose my half-cooked meal made me totally forget the bullets flying by. When we had gone a little way, my master and I reached into the pot and ate hastily with our fingers. Because of the cold, we couldn't uncover our hands. . . .

When day broke, we stood near the stream approximately 1,000 paces from the two wooden bridges built near each other. They were like sloping saw-horses suspended like trestles on shallow-sunk piles. On these lay long stringers and across them unfastened bridge ties. One could not see the bridges because of the crowd of people, horses, and wagons. Everyone crowded together into a solid mass. Nowhere could one see a way out or a means of rescue. From morning till night we were at the mercy of the cannonballs and grenades which the Russians hurled at us from two sides. At each blow, three to five men were struck down, but no one could move a step to avoid the cannonballs. Only by filling the space where a cannonball made room could one inch forward. The powder wagons stood in the crowd. Many were ignited by grenades, killing hundreds of people and horses around them.

I had one horse to ride and another to lead. I soon had to release the horse I led and had to kneel on the other to prevent my feet from being crushed, for everything was so closely packed that in fifteen minutes one could advance only four or five steps. To be on foot was to lose all hope of salvation. Whoever lacked a good mount fell over the masses of sprawling people and horses. Everyone was screaming under their hooves, and everywhere were cries of "Shoot me or stab me to death!" The fallen horses knocked down many of those still standing. It was a miracle that anyone survived.

In the crowd the Major and I held each other tightly. As far as possible, I made my horse rear up and come down again about one step further forward. I was astounded at the intelligence this animal used to save us. Then evening came, and despair increased. Thousands swam into the river with horses, but no one came out again. Thousands of others near the water were pushed in. The stream was like a sheep dip where the heads of men and horses bobbed and disappeared.

Finally, around 4 p.m., when almost dark, I reached the bridge. There was only one bridge, the second having been shot away. Today it is with horror, but at the time with dull indifference, that I see the masses of horses and people lying dead, piled high upon the bridge. I told myself: "Straight ahead and in the middle! . . . The water is your grave; across the bridge is the continuation of a wretched life. The decision will be made on the bridge!" I kept myself steadily in the middle. The Major and I helped one another. So, amid 100 saber blows we came to the bridge, where not a plank was visible because of the dead men and horses. Although people fell in masses on reaching the bridge, 30 paces to the right and left, we reached firm land.

The bridge was covered with horses and men not only because of shooting and falling, but also the loose bridge ties. The horses stepped between them and fell, until the planks were held down by the weight of their bodies. Wherever a plank remained loose, it was dislodged by the falling horses, creating a trap for the next horse. The weight of the dead bodies saved those riding across; for, without their load, the cannon would have destroyed the bridge too soon.

When I finally reached safety, it was dark. I did not know where the highway was. I lay down to the left of the road in a little clump of bushes and tied the horses to my foot. The Major gave a Pole a coin to fetch water with a kettle purchased the day before, but man and kettle were never seen again, and we both had to eat snow to quench our thirst. There were now so few people around that in our quiet place it seemed as though everyone had died. The cannon fire also ceased, and the bridge had sunk. The fate of the people still on the other side was horrible: hunger, cold, and water brought them death. . . .

I could look indifferently at the people falling by hundreds, although their heads smashed on the ice. I could look at their rising and falling again, their dull moaning and whining, and the wringing and clenching of their hands. The ice and snow sticking in their mouths was frightful. Yet I felt no pity. I thought only of my friends.

By the end of December, we reached the Polish border along the Niemen River. . . . I led my horse up it and crossed. It was filled with pieces of ice. Pieces 15 to 18 inches thick drifted by, extremely difficult to avoid. Here the Polish army turned left onto the Warsaw highway. I and many other Germans did too. Everyone believed the enemy would not pursue the Poles on this route and that we would be safe. But eager to rob and plunder, the enemy did not stop even here. Even the Poles robbed and plundered the Germans and French, as I discovered the same evening.

That evening a mounted troop came and said, "Comrade, stay with us!" I said, "That's fine with me." When we had gone a little further, they attacked some of the soldiers and took their horses and belongings. When I saw this, I turned my horse and fled as fast as I could. They did not catch me, since just then a troop of Westphalian[4] infantry approached, which I joined. I expected to travel on with them. When dusk fell, however, we looked for a village, but did not see one. Finally, some lights twinkled from across the Niemen. We decided to cross back; hunger and cold made us heedless of the danger, and we believed that the enemy was far away.

It really was a village. For the first time since leaving Moscow, I entered a decent house, where we were warm and could buy bread and brandy. There were 10 of us, and the villagers seemed harmless. At last, at about 10 p.m., two peasants asked for bullets to go rabbit-hunting.

The Westphalians still had muskets and powder, and gave them bullets. Hardly an hour had passed before a band of peasants burst in, seized those lying on the floor, and took their guns. I saw no chance for help and thought, besides, that these were Russian peasants, brutal enough to commit murder.

---

[4] Westphalia was a German state allied with Napoleonic France.

The lights went out. In a flash, I took my hat under my fur and left, took my horse which was standing tied and unbridled by the door, and rode away wildly over fences and snowdrifts. . . .

I was alone and free. When I spotted a trail, I rode as fast as possible, for the noise from the village was so loud that I feared I might still be caught. I rode as fast as possible over the cracks in the ice across the Niemen River to get to the Polish side. Early in the morning, I entered a little town full of Germans, Frenchmen, and Poles. Nevertheless, I was able to get some bread. . . .

I hurried on, taking the highway between Königsberg and Warsaw to Thorn. It was thronged with Germans and Frenchmen. Until now there had been no hope of finding lodgings, and food could only be procured by money or force. One day I came to a nobleman's estate where I asked for bread and was given not only bread but also butter and brandy by a German-speaking servant. He asked my nationality and the name of my home town or village. I told him everything, that I was Catholic and that my country's late ruler had been a Polish prince. This greatly pleased him. When Poles learned you were Catholic, they esteemed you more highly than others. I was given several things to eat along the way; but when I looked for my horse, it was already gone. Only as a particular favor from the nobleman did I recover it. Nearly everyone who came alone with a horse had it taken.

Several days later, while I drank a brandy at an inn, my horse, which I had tied by the front door, was stolen. I searched the houses and stables in vain, so found myself on foot. Until now my feet had been wrapped with woolen cloth over my shoes, but it weighed so much that it hindered walking. Every morning as soon as I was outdoors, I had to run energetically for an hour. I thought it would be impossible to keep my feet from freezing.

With eight German comrades I proceeded toward Ordensburg, where the road led through a wood that took almost three hours to traverse.

Here the Poles had formed robber bands dressed in Cossack outfits with sabers, pistols, and other arms. A gang actually came and grabbed me, one to my right, one to my left, the third pressing a saber against my chest. My comrades ahead were left alone, because they looked more like beggar Jews than I. The robbers tore off my fur, coat, cape, vests, and head cloths, threw me down, and were about to take my boots, too. Meanwhile they found my money, 18 rubles, in my cape pocket. This saved me: had they not found the money, I would have been left to freeze to death unclothed. As it was, however, they dropped the coat and cape, along with one of the two vests, and went off with the money, the fur, the other vest, and two head cloths. During this time my comrades kept hidden in the distance. When they saw I was free, they ran back and dressed me, for I was so stiff that I couldn't dress myself.

That same evening I reached Ordensburg and for the first time was given regular quarters. From there I went on to Niklawi and received quarters again. It was Christmas Eve, which I would not have known had I not learned it from the landlord. Here I washed myself for the first time, but could not get rid of my lice. . . .

The washing of my hands and face proceeded very slowly because the crust on my hands, ears, and nose had grown like fir-bark, with cracks and coal black scales. My face resembled that of a heavily bearded Russian peasant. When I looked into the mirror, I was astonished at its strange appearance. I washed for an hour with hot water and soap. However, I only became somewhat smoother and lighter, but did not notice any lessening of the blackness and scales. Only where I had not been shaving did somewhat lighter skin appear. . . .

Spending the night in the cold again gave me a fever. The next day I had to continue on foot alone, but toward evening it became impossible. Either to die on the way or go off to a village I spotted from the highway—that was my only choice. I decided to go into the village. I went into a room and immediately lay on the floor, where the fever shook me frightfully. The people wanted to give me food and spirits, but I could drink nothing but water. The onlookers made gestures of hopelessness. I naturally could not understand their speech, but I sensed their pity. In the morning I mustered my last strength, left my arms behind because I was so weak, and only toward evening did I arrive in the station-town two hours away, where I found my convoy had already marched off again. I did not seek lodging from the quartering office, but lay down in a tavern where there were two Westphalian soldiers who also had the fever at its worst stage. . . .

The next day a citizen of the town came to the inn and asked what ailed us three. He could speak German. We answered that we had the fever. "The fever?" he said. "I can help you get rid of that." This he really did, sitting down, writing three notes, and saying we should each eat one, however we liked to eat it. I, at least, had little faith that it would help. Nevertheless, I ate mine and, when the time came for me to be shaken again, I waited longer and longer, and actually the fever left not only me but also my other two comrades at the same time. This seemed miraculous and delightful to all of us. We thanked this good man, without whom we would have died. The next day, when we could eat again, we obtained a wagon from the police, and I reached the convoy again outside the city of Posen. However, I could no longer walk.

The march continued through Posen toward Crossen. It was still extraordinarily cold. Since I could not walk, I froze terribly. Also, at night we came into the most miserable huts where even the healthy had a hard time bearing the cold and smoke in the earthen-floor rooms. The convoy numbered 175 men. However, one or two died daily. Our food was still inadequate, and there was no medicine. Although the groaning and shrieking on the wagons continued without interruption, and several of the severely ill were crushed to death by the healthier people, since the space on the wagons was so small, the impulse to help one another remained quite dulled. . . .

It was still 250 hours to home; my homecoming was still uncertain. Nevertheless, hope gave me strength. I finally reached Crossen, Torgau, and Leipzig, where German life began again. Decent food and warm rooms increased my strength somewhat. . . .

My convoy had left behind 100 dead. . . . Since people here already knew of our arrival . . . my brother and brother-in-law, Herr Wagner, hurried toward Rettstadt to look for me. I suddenly saw them. They would not have recognized me, as I looked then. But I called, thrust out my hand, and greeted them. They jumped for joy and squeezed my hands. Our hearts alone could feel, for we could not speak. Oh, that everyone might know how high the love of friends and relatives can rise at such a chance meeting! One feels in it heavenly joy, the all-wise providence of God, and at the same time the miracle of nature.

My brother-in-law immediately ran with powerful strides toward the town and announced my arrival. Thus I made my entrance with a sooty Russian coat, an old round hat, and countless traveling companions, including Russians, Poles, Prussians, and Saxons, in and under my clothing. I stopped at my very good friend the innkeeper's. Everyone wanted to lift me down and lead me. Everyone regarded me as weaker than I really was. However, I stayed only a few minutes in the room before I removed my clothes in the hay loft, put on new ones provided for me, and washed myself. Only then was I fit for clean company.

I also awaited my dear sisters, who came from Rosenberg the next day and were another object of joy. The sincere joy of meeting again kindled the love of family like a divine flame. Now the wish was fulfilled for which they had shed so many tears and so often prayed to God.

The next day, Shrove Thursday, a holiday was observed at the innkeeper's request. He brought it about through the city commandant, Alberti, who often came to the tavern. I now had good eating and drinking, but my stomach could not stand much. I always had to be careful. On the third day, when we had driven on again, we came to Schorndorf at night and were shut together in a house to prevent spreading sickness, for everywhere in Würrtemberg we were shunned like lepers. When we came to Waiblingen, the convoy was divided. Those in better health, of whom I was one, went to Waldenbuch. Those whose health was worse went to Vahingen-on-the-Enz. After a fortnight I was dispatched as a convalescent to Asberg and incorporated into the sharpshooters stationed there. I marched out several times with them. Barely four days had passed, however, before the fever shook me again, although it did not break out. I ran a high temperature. My nosebleed grew so bad that for several days a wet cloth had to be put around my head and neck every five or six minutes, and the bed had to be arranged for sitting up instead of lying down. Since my illness worsened, I was examined by the general army physician and was granted leave. . . . An invalid's pension was also promised.

When I had grown so weak that I became delirious and everyone doubted that I would recover, I was loaded on a wagon with several "Russians" and driven to Vahingen. I was now so weak that I had to be lifted on and off the wagon and could take nothing but water. In Vahingen I was laid immediately in the room where the dying were brought. I couldn't keep down medicine or food. However, the bleeding had stopped.

Finally, after eight or nine days, I craved vinegar, and poured some into my soup. These few spoonfuls of soup stayed down, and my desire for vinegar and lettuce increased. The lettuce also stayed down, although I had to eat it secretly without the doctor's knowing about it. My appetite gradually grew so that I had potato salad, pure vinegar, pork, potatoes and cabbage, and cooked meat brought to me secretly from the butcher. I stopped taking medicine. I attribute my recovery to bleedings, which purged my corrupted blood, and vinegar, which washed off the encrusted lining in my body, cleaned my blood, and revived my appetite.

When my relatives and friends heard of my illness, my little sister, greatly worried, came to visit me. . . . When I saw her and she saw me, it took a long time for her to stop weeping and speak. My appearance frightened her terribly, for I was deathly pale, my coat was bloody, and my voice, deep and weak. But, when I said that I thought myself out of danger, since I felt almost well and could eat everything, she was somewhat comforted. . . .

For two-weeks I still had violent attacks of gout in the soles of my feet, as well as a bad headache. But I did not take my medicine and always told the physician that I was well. However, he did not believe me and said I must have a headache and gout in my feet. I agreed with him, but only in my thoughts.

Finally, I was brought with about 70 men to Waldenbuch to the convalescent hospital and was quartered along the way in a village. For fear of the nervous fever, we were quarantined in the town hall. This was hard on us, always to be treated like lepers. . . .

At Waldenbuch Castle I more or less got my strength back, since I bought what I wanted to supplement my regular diet. Then I wrote to Lieutenant Stimmer at Asberg, asking him to help me get my promised discharge. This was done. . . .

I immediately went through Stuttgart toward Asberg. But at the first village in the direction of Ludwigsburg, I suddenly got such pain in my foot that I had to walk an hour instead of a quarter hour to get to the village. Several people who saw me and recognized me as a "Russian"—as everyone who had been there was then called—gave me presents. Finally I reached the mayor's house and was taken to Asberg. I obtained my discharge and had myself driven home, where I soon became entirely healthy and well.

9

FRIEDERICH LUDWIG BURK

Diary

1806–1816

Friederich Ludwig Burk (1787–1866) was a prosperous farmer from Wiesbaden, capital of the western German principality of Nassau-Usingen, which, like Württemberg, was allied with Napoleon. His father's family had worked as stewards of princely lands, an occupation that barred them from Wiesbaden citizenship because employees of the princes were not thought to have the ordinary townsfolk's interests at heart. His mother came from an old Wiesbaden family whose members regularly held municipal office.

In 1776, Burk's father left his princely employment and became a citizen, integrating the family into the municipal elite. Like most well-to-do

Das Tagebuch des Friederich Ludwig Burk: Aufzeichnungen eines Wiesbadener Bürgers und Bauern, 1806–1866, ed. Jochen Dollwet and Thomas Weichel (Wiesbaden: Schriften des Stadtarchivs Wiesbaden, 1993), 41–98.

farmers, Burk pursued many economic activities, including agriculture and property speculation, but he specialized in transporting goods by cart—a lucrative occupation given Wiesbaden's rapid growth. He did not wed until 1833, when he married the widow of his older brother, Johann Friederich, who had died in 1828. A son was born a few months after the marriage. At about the same time, Burk edited the diary he had been keeping sporadically since 1806, producing the "polished" version excerpted here. The original has not survived. It is not clear why Burk decided to reinvigorate his diary at this point. Perhaps it had something to do with his marriage and the birth of his son. In any case, it offers unique insight into the worldview of a wealthy farmer living through the Napoleonic Wars. For him, as for many other civilians, war was an unpleasant intrusion into the normal course of his life, disrupting his business affairs, household, and family life—often with tragic results.

1806

After the peace [treaty] of 1805 between the emperor of Austria and the Emperor Napoleon,[1] from the beginning of 1806, the French army was spread all over our country. We suffered much from billeting and requisitions. Our prince had to kowtow to the emperor, and was declared a sovereign prince in the Confederation of the Rhine in August. Immediately after the title was conferred, war with Prussia was declared, and our country had to provide four battalions of support troops. Recruits were drawn from all over the country, even from cities which had previously been exempt. Even our city of Wiesbaden was going to have to give up the right of exemption it had purchased and furnish troops. But because there was so much opposition, it remained free, and only illegitimate sons and the sons of inhabitants without citizenship rights were conscripted and marched toward Prussia in November.

It was a mild winter, a dry early summer and a wet harvest season, a beautiful Indian summer and autumn, mild till New Year.

1807

The winter was very mild, spring warm and wet, summer very hot, autumn pleasant.

---

[1] The Peace of Pressburg (December 25, 1805).

The crops developed well. Even the fruit. The meadow on the Salz is being turned into fields and gardens. A gardener from Sachsenhausen called Fetz leased the large lordly meadow on the Salz River, developed it into a garden, and is having a small house built there. The school was enlarged by one floor. The wall of our garden bordering the stream was repaired in March. It cost 20 gulden in wages for the mason, 11 tubs of lime, each tub costing 1 gulden.[2] A new feed trough was installed along the whole length of the cowshed. This summer the salt [monopoly] was leased to Mr. Führer. He sells it by the pound, and nobody else is allowed to sell any. Even itinerant salt merchants are forbidden. The mill stream was enclosed in an iron channel in front of the criminal jail and court.

The forest was divided up, and the last wood-gathering day in the communal forest was in November. We were allotted only half of our usual amount of wood and, instead of the other half, we were assigned old oak trees. The pond on the Warmen dike was drained and turned into a cabbage field. Fire insurance was introduced. The orphans were removed from the orphanage and distributed among the citizens. The orphanage was rented out. In autumn we had a new gate with a small superstructure attached to our house, a threshold built, the gable to the street cut off, and the house repaired in other ways. We had a hen with chicks already in February, and these chicks were already laying eggs by harvest season. At the end of the year, a wolf was shot in the forest on Trompeter Hill.

Preparations are being made to construct the spa complex. Timber was collected in late autumn. Until then, the forest was held in common by the city and villages. Every Monday and Thursday were wood-gathering days, when everybody could gather as much dry and dead wood as he wanted. Even old trees could be cut down, which were then taxed at less than their value; if a cartload was charged 15 kreutzer, and a tree produced six cartloads, then instead of paying 90 kreutzer, you only had to pay 45.[3] . . . The winter was bearable and mild, spring warm and wet, summer very warm, autumn pleasant.

1808

Some of the Nassau[4] soldiers who had fought against the Prussians returned on January 1st, and most were infected with scabies. Since the 1st of January, every butcher has to offer all types of meat. Until now,

---

[2] At the time, unskilled laborers earned approximately 100 to 150 gulden annually.
[3] Forty-five kreutzer then represented two to three days' wages for an unskilled laborer.
[4] A small German state allied with Napoleon.

they had been divided into four categories, of which one, consisting of five butchers, slaughtered only oxen. Four others slaughtered calves, four pigs, and four rams. Every few years, they changed categories and did not allow new master butchers into their guild. The oxen butchers all stuck together, and only one of them had meat at any given time. The next one would not start offering meat until the first one had sold out. They all grew rich that way.

These butcher regulations were all revoked, and everybody could slaughter whatever he wanted, however he wanted. The baker Weik ran away on February 16th while on his way to Kaub, and Mr. Ackermann of the Schützenhoff estate fell off his horse on the 19th by the Armenruh mill and broke his neck.

On March 4th, three Jews were hung at the gallows. They had murdered a butcher from Höchst. Although the Jewish community offered to pay much money, they were kept hanging until the evening of the 7th. The winter has been relatively cold so far. The sale of fields from [the prince's] Köppersteinigen estate has begun. Sheep have been forbidden to pasture on the meadows, and people are being urged to get rid of them entirely.

At the beginning of April, a census was taken of the number of inhabitants and dogs. The construction of the spa complex is proceeding fast. We had a hard freeze on the 20th, and on the 22nd of April we had a shower while it was cold and raw. In the beginning of May we received the first new princely copper kreutzer. Privy councilor Thelenius is beginning to build a house in Frederick Street. . . . It only began to get warm at the beginning of May. By the 12th, the grain began to have ears. . . .

On the 22nd a new girder was placed along the length of the barn roof.

On May 14th, we had been able to sow beet seeds on a field, and on June 23rd we were already able to transplant the seedlings. On July 10th everybody was allowed to butcher animals and sell the meat. The communal forest is being surveyed, and its limits marked out with cut and other stones. Again, recruits were supposed to be drawn from among the children of the citizens, but it was dropped because of opposition.

Talk is of war.

14th August. The upper wing of the spa complex collapsed, but fortunately at 4 a.m. when no workers were about.

On August 21st, two battalions of Nassau troops marched towards Spain, which began a war with France. The side of our house facing the street was modified, new walls were put in, new windows too, and the high gable was cut off. On November 20th, there was unease among the citizens because soldiers were to be conscripted by lottery from among the sons of the townsfolk, so they turned again to the prince for help.

In early December, we received the new princely silver coin, a 6-kreutzer piece. On the 16th of December, all the young men of the town finally had to be measured, and then I requested a medical certificate about my chest from privy councilor Lehr. After December 25th, young men under 24 were not supposed to become citizens.[5]

Spring was raw and cold this year, especially April when it was still freezing. Yet it was a fertile and good year. There was much fruit and plums, crops, potatoes, beets, hay, and straw.

1809

The calendars for this year were subjected to a stamp tax, and we had to pay more for them.

February. Talk is about war against Austria. Great numbers of French occupation troops marched out of Hanover[6] against Austria.

Those with carts are being forced to do much compulsory labor on the spa complex.

February. The old Herren garden outside the Sonnenberg Gate was partly leveled.

On February 14th, at 8 p.m. during Carnival, we had two rain showers. One moved over the Rhine, and the other over the forest.

There is lots of construction happening in Nero Street.

March. The city had to furnish its first four soldiers, but instead of drawing lots among the sons of the citizens, it provided four paid men. Lorenz Zollinger, Finzens Roos, Friedrich Dehn, and Seewald all received 300 gulden. . . .

Every young man, who marries now and has not already been a soldier, will have to pay 5 gulden for every 100 gulden of his wealth.

A rural police force was established.

This year it was a very nice March. Everything is beginning to turn green and grow.

April. The 1st Nassau regiment marched toward Austria on the 8th. It is rumored that the tax rates are going to be changed and that there will be a new tax imposed on fields and trades.

---

[5] Citizenship exempted one from military service.
[6] A German state possessed by England. France had occupied it early in the war.

May. The first house frames have gone up in Nero Street.

There is a lot of opposition to sheep, and they were supposed to be eliminated. On May 18th they had to be removed from the fields, but because of their owners' opposition, they went back out on the 20th.

28th May. The towns of Bierstadt and Erbenheim are being forced to pay the new tax.

June 4th. Five citizens of Bierstadt were arrested at daybreak because they opposed the new tax.

On the 10th of the same month, two citizens of Rambach and two of Naurod were arrested because they would not accept the valuation of their fields.

12th June. There is indescribably lovely clover on the field.

July. Every day four men from the town visit the fields to evaluate them and divide them into different categories.

In Flörssheim the new tax was forcibly collected.

September. The city is attempting to repurchase its privileges and exemptions, and is demanding 16 kreutzer from every citizen.

The night watchmen are no longer allowed to trumpet the time, but only to call it out.

October. Today on the 8th, pastor Handel said his last sermon; song 478 of the hymn book, the text Ephesians, chapter 4, verses 22 to 28.

There is peace again with Austria.[7]

November. [My brother] Joh[ann] Heinrich joined the rural police.

A new road through Erbenheim to Frankfurt is being planned.

Today, November 19th, pastor Heidenreich held his first sermon: his text was Romans 15, verses 19 to the end. Songs were 538 and 236.

Pastoral candidate Krim of Erbenheim was invested and became the assistant of Inspector Koch.

On December 10th a peace festival was held, the sermon was given by pastor Heidenreich; the prescribed text is in Jeremiah 29, verses 11 to 14, song 547 was sung.

On the 13th I brought a keg of honey from Walauf to pharmacist Lade.

Now we are at year's end. When it began, who could have imagined that the foundations of such an exorbitant burden of taxation were going to be laid.

The price of timber has gone up to 10 gulden per cord.

The crop ripened relatively well, but there was little fruit.

---

[7] The Peace of Schönbrunn (October 14, 1809).

1810

14th January. The first Nassau regiment, which had been in Austria, crossed the Rhine at Mannheim and marched toward Spain.

The new road to Erbenheim was begun; all transportation and labor is being furnished by corvée.[8]

10th February. A [military] lottery was held among the sons of the citizens for the first time, since the city has to provide four men.

On May 3rd, food was served for the first time in the spa complex.

On the night of the 29th to the 30th, the beans and potatoes were killed by frost.

On September 23rd, candidate Krim gave his farewell sermon.

October 7th. Superintendent-General Müler of Weilburg gave his first sermon; his text was Romans 15, verse 29, and songs 233 and 538.

High taxes were imposed on foreign goods.

November 23rd and 24th. Many English goods were burned at the local marketplace. This was repeated several more times in December.

The night watchmen are trumpeting the time again.

The city gates are being torn down. This year several houses were built in Lower Frederick Street, and many more in the Nero Street.

Everything grew relatively well, but there was little fruit.

The war in Spain continues.

1811

January. The New Gate of the town near the orphanage is being pulled down. They began digging for gravel on our field near the old stream; it is being used for the paths in front of the spa complex.

On January 19th, I was at the town hall for our property assessment under the new tax.

In Lower Frederick Street, everyone with carts is having one requisitioned and is being forced to carry cobblestones with it.

War with Russia is expected.

10th February. Another 280 men from Nassau marched toward Spain.

Two old brickyard huts and the potters' huts in front of Sonneberg Gate were pulled down and rebuilt in the Nero Street.

The 26th. On Carnival I undertook a very cumbersome walk to get an ox and arrived back home only at 11 p.m. because of the mud. I saw big fiery balls flying, and down at the Bierstadt Road above the Pletz mill

---

[8] Forced labor service.

I saw two will-o'-the-wisps in the shape of men, who were beating each other so hard that sparks flew.

The weather was relatively mild.

March. The brickyard huts have been begun in the Nero Street.

17th. We have delivered 1 1/8 perches[9] of paving stones with one pair of oxen under compulsory labor to pave the lower Frederick Street; the stones had to be got from the forest on Sleepy-Head Hill or elsewhere, where those with a cart could find suitable stones. The sand too is being brought by corvée from Hessler, Mossbach, and elsewhere.

Many crippled soldiers are returning from Spain.

April. The mill stream, which until now had flowed openly through the lower Weber Alley, is now being covered up with boards.

2nd. Blackthorn and cherries are flowering.

14th. Pear trees and linseed are flowering.

21st. Apple trees are flowering.

28th. The pond behind the spa complex is being filled with water for the first time. . . .

May 6th a lottery was held again, and Jo[hann] Fr[iederich] has n[umber] 16.

Different houses are being built in the Nero Street.

19th. The sheep were shorn.

Salt Stream, along the Erbenheim highway, is being enclosed. . . .

June 2nd. The grapes are flowering. The linseed is early.

On June 12th/14th grass is already being cut for hay.

Senior clerk Ebel and Ph[ilip] Traub are building houses in the lower Frederick Street. Traub is beginning to put up the wood frame.

30th. Grain is early. The weather was warm in June.

July. Construction has begun on the houses of Gottfried Hahn, brickyard owner Rizel, and Balthaser Schlink in the Nero Street.

14th. We had some very warm weather, the heat was seven degrees [celsius] higher than anyone could have imagined.

20th to the 21st there were heavy showers with hail and much flooding. Water got into the spa complex.

21st. The wheat is early and is being harvested. The weather is nice again.

August 4th. We had rainy days and could not harvest all week long. The barley is beginning to grow and had to be partly turned over.

9th. The lads chosen by the lottery on May 16th were supposed to be drafted, but most are unfit.

---

[9] A perch was a unit of measurement a bit longer than sixteen feet.

The weather is good again, and they brought in barley and oats through the 18th.

The new road to Erbenheim is now being graveled from the town onward.

On the 26th work was done on the vineyard hills.

September. A dance floor is being added to the Waldmühle inn. People are beginning to gather fruit and nuts.

8th. A comet was visible over the forest in the direction of the Geissberg.

15th. Potatoes are being gathered.

29th. This week the very first new trade tax was levied.

October. October 8th was autumn or grape harvest. The wine this year is excellent and there is also a lot of it.

The weather is still nice.

November 15th. Another 500 Nassau army recruits marched off to Spain.

Now they are planting fruit trees on both sides of the road to Erbenheim. They are being planted by a gardener, and every big landowner has to pay 3 kreutzer per pole, tree, and for the planting fee.

Behind the spa complex, the grounds are being laid out.

December. The forest is being surveyed and will be taxed.

December 15th. The very first land tax is being imposed and collected.

The prince gave away many Christmas presents. To his minister, he gave the Bierstadt estate and fields. To tax director Vigelius, he gave the secularized nunnery. He also gave things to the general and many others.

In this year almost everything developed well, especially the wine, many plums, and other good fruit.

Everything ripened earlier and was of better quality.

1812

January 13th we traded a quarter of a beef and 47 pounds of cow hide for tanner Michel's windmill and, since he is also giving 3 gulden and a fur, the mill costs a total of 13 gulden.

Another four townsmen became soldiers.

The 19th. There is talk of a new war with Russia.

On the 20th our cabbage field behind the hospital, on the 22nd the field on the Warmen dike and the first one on the Salz were all turned into building sites and gardens.

February 20th. I was bled for the first time.[10] In the Nero Street different houses were begun.

April 5th. A small tower was built on top of the Catholic church. We are breaking in our young bulls to the harness.

The 12th. Another 700 army recruits marched off to Spain.

April 17th. We received 312 gulden 39 kreutzer for a part of the field behind the hospital which was turned into building sites, and 10 gulden for the tree on it.

The 26th. The house of Elmer built on our field in the Nero Street and many similar houses were begun.

May 3rd. The price of grain has risen steeply, a malter[11] costs 12 to 13 gulden. A malter of wheat, about 170 pounds, is 21 to 23 gulden.

The 10th. The grain is beginning to get ears.

The French emperor is moving with his army to Russia and crossed the Rhine this week.

The 24th. The night was so cold that the beans and potatoes froze in the fields.

The 27th. The field on the Warmen dike is being paid for, 219 gulden 48 kreutzer.

May 31st. Different houses in the Frederick Street, also the first house on the Pletz mill, were framed. The Nassau Inn and, facing it, the house of Zais are being built outside of Sonneberg Gate. . . .

June 1st. We sowed barley on the Bierstadt Road field.

On the 27th one of the princesses drowned herself. She was melancholic.

The crops are being harvested. The price of grain continues to fall.

July 14th. The Jew Mayer hanged himself in tailor Todt's house.

On the 30th we brought home the first grain.

August 23rd. A very heavy sum of money was demanded for the upkeep of the street lamps; we had to pay 22 gulden as our part.

October 3rd. There is talk about the construction of a barracks.

October 10th. We celebrated a victory feast because of the big victories of the French in Russia.[12] In the evening the main streets of the town were illuminated. The prince, his wife and princess, and all the servants went to the local church. There were so many people that its upper supports had to be strengthened.

---

[10] At the time, bloodletting was commonly used to treat the sick. Burk does not indicate from what illness he was suffering.

[11] About forty-seven gallons.

[12] The Battle of Borodino (September 7, 1812) and the occupation of Moscow a week later (September 14, 1812).

The 17th. According to the news, the French were beaten in Spain and are retreating.

The 28th was autumn, the wine is bad.

November 6th. Another 700 recruits from Nassau are marching toward Spain.

8th. The field that was used for the new road to Erbenheim is being paid for; we received 76 gulden 52 kreutzer 2 pennies for our two plots.

The 15th. There is talk that the French were beaten in Russia and are retreating.

December 9th. Our first plot on the Salz is being purchased by Führer for 10 gulden per niederschlag,[13] for a total of 450 gulden. The title deed cost 4 gulden and many kreutzer.

We sold both our bulls for 14 carolins[14] because we were concerned about the war. The French in Russia are supposed to be in the most wretched condition. Many thousands of men and most of their horses are said to have frozen to death. 1812 was a cold, raw year; nonetheless, most things grew, but not much fruit.

Taxes were raised five times.

Because there was so much construction, we had to do a lot of forced labor with our cart.

At the Waldmühl inn, a big hall was built.

1813

One fears a sad year because of the horrible military events everywhere; whether the French are victorious or defeated, either way it will be bad for us.

The blood-tenth,[15] which had previously only been imposed on sheep here, has been replaced by a new tax. For every lamb that is still in arrears for last year's blood-tenth, one must pay 18 kreutzer to the tax collector.

Burg Street has been opened.

Many Frenchmen are crossing the Rhine to join the army in Prussia.

February 8th. The lower piece of land on the old stream next to my godfather's, where they had dug for gravel to use at the spa, is being purchased for 184 gulden 41 kreutzer. The cost per niederschlag is 3 gulden 45 kreutzer.

[13] Approximately sixteen feet.
[14] A gold coin worth eleven gulden.
[15] A tax on livestock.

The weather was relatively mild so far.

On the 23rd the whole gravel pit on the old stream was relinquished and auctioned off. We bought it back for 93 gulden.

There is much construction in the upper Frederick Street opposite the New Alley.

March 8th. We sold the rest of our cabbage field behind the hospital to shoemaker Elmer at the assessed price, 6 gulden 30 kreutzer per niederschlag.

On the 14th another 600 army recruits from Nassau marched off to Spain.

I planted five good cherry trees among the trees on our plum field.

The 21st. Many Frenchmen are marching to the army in Prussia.

There is much work at Kassel and Mainz on the entrenchments.

We have to deliver paving-stones again, as part of our forced-labor obligation.

April 4th. The construction of the little palace on the corner of Frederick and William Streets near the Pletz mill has begun.

We have begun working to turn the old stream gravel pit into a field.

The Russian army is supposed to have advanced far; dreadful battles have occurred between them and the French.

May 2nd. Pastor Heidenreich gave his final sermon and moved to Dotzheim.

Austria has joined the Russian army and declared war on France.

On the 30th Pastor Schellenberg gave his first sermon.

June 6th. There is supposed to be a truce between Russia and Prussia with the French.[16]

On the 13th another victory feast was celebrated. The price of grain has dropped somewhat. Wheat costs 10 gulden 20 kreutzer.

The wool sold for 36 kreutzer per pound.

July 24th. The new pharmacy in the Golden Wolf inn, now known as the Lion pharmacy, opposite the bathhouse and Eagle inn, was opened for the first time.

The truce was extended, but both armies are rearming frantically; uncountable Frenchmen are moving toward the army in Saxony. The Russian army is growing just as fast, and in Prussia everyone is said to be taking up arms. Frightful battles are feared.

According to the news from Spain, the Nassau troops have suffered heavily and lost many men.

---

[16]The Truce of Poischwitz (June 4, 1813).

July. This year the city council bought off the ten percent tax on crops for 760 malter. . . .

August. Construction began this week on Kässebir's and Zollinger's stables at the stream behind our garden. My mother gave them permission to extend their sheds one and a half feet, as far as their rainspouts, but had to have their gables oriented toward the stream.

On the 21st Kässebir dared to break down our wall in order to enclose the stream at that point, which led to a formal legal complaint. Expert witnesses allowed him to build a 4-foot-wide stable over the stream, but it must not touch our wall and has to be one and a half feet away from it.

August. Austria is with Russia against the French.

September 6th. The estates of the Köpperstein farm have been auctioned off; we acquired two 30-acre plots along the Schierstein Road.

The 10th a carpenter died at the construction site of the palace near the Pletz mill, when he was hit on the head by a heavy plank which had been thrown down by the other carpenters. Seven carpenters had been carrying this piece of wood for the frame on the lower floor. Six were carrying it on their left shoulders, and the seventh on his right. When they threw it down, it hit the seventh on the head.

In the upper Frederick Street many houses have been framed.

October 6th. Wounded Frenchmen are coming through the town and being driven to Mainz.

Church Alley is being connected with Frederick Street through the gardens and city wall. The Foul Stream will be enclosed.

Houses are being built in the William Street. The field is horribly full of mice.

October. Bavaria and Württemberg joined the allies.

Attempts are being made to get the Kissel Spring to flow into the town.

The 29th was autumn and grape-gathering.

The French are now in full retreat. We don't notice it too much here, but from Frankfurt all the way to Hochheim and Mainz the streets are teeming with them. This week straggling regiments, some unarmed and others without horses, passed through Idstein to Mainz.

November 2nd. The last French we had to billet left. We survived their retreat quite happily.

The 4th around 11 o'clock lunchtime, the first Cossacks,[17] five to six of them, came through the town from the direction of the Platt, and continued through to Bierstadt. One of them was shot dead by the French.

---

[17] Russian light cavalry.

Austrian hussars and uhlans,[18] together with some Tyrolian Jägers, arrived in the afternoon. Several hundred men spent the night in and around Moss Stream.

The 5th. 5,000 Cossacks arrived and set up camp outside town either on Michel's Hill or in front of Heather Hill. Bread and brandy, wood and forage, were brought to them. In addition, they took a lot of wood, bean-poles, tree trunks, and kindling from the town and its environs, built themselves straw huts, and stayed the night.

Already by the 14th, my mother had to give them 27 hundred-weights of hay and 56 bales of straw.

On the 11th the entire Cossack corps arrived. The whole town was full of them. There were horses tied up in every house and shed, and even on the streets at bakeries where they had to be fed by the shop-keepers. There were straw huts erected in the marketplace, huge fires burning, people cooking, whole rows of horses tied up there and being fed. The fields just outside town, from the spa complex over the field to the Bierstadt Road, from that road to the Erbenheim highway to the Han bridge, and from there to the new mill, were even more full of Cossacks, with whole lanes of straw huts. Hay and straw, bread and livestock, were brought to them.

The 15th the Prussians appeared, but the Cossacks who were sup-posed to move on, remained. Because they did not receive any more food and forage, they helped themselves from the surrounding villages: hay, grain, and straw, cattle and sheep, indeed everything they could find. They even cut down all the saplings along the Erbenheim highway.

More and more Prussians arrived, and on the 17th the Cossacks fi-nally moved on to Frankfurt via Erbenheim.

The state of their encampment was indescribable. It was strewn with dead and half-dead horses, the intestines and hides of slaughtered live-stock, pitchers, bottles, and pots of butter, cheese, plum butter, honey, beehives, flour, apples, nuts, whole heaps of spoiled hay, sheaves of grain, ladders, crockery and firewood, poles, sheepskins, whole and cut up sacks that they had received full of oats, dried meats—all taken from our region.

On leaving, they burned their straw huts.

The 22nd. The town is now full of Prussians: my mother has 16 of them billeted on her. Up to now, she has had to furnish 30½ hundred weights of hay. The town council searched for oats in the attic, and she had to turn over one more big sack.

---

[18] German light cavalry.

The 24th. She now has 24 men billeted on her, and often an additional six to eight show up at night.

The 25th. We had to deliver hay, straw, and oats. Those without oats had to give grain.

Our prince has to provide auxiliary troops, and the militia battalions came to Usingen and many recruits went there.

November 30th. My brother Joh[ann] Heinrich was summoned for militia service with his company; this brought my mother great sorrow.

December 1st. The whole house is full of soldiers, the stables of horses. Tonight there were another five Prussian uhlan horses tied up in the courtyard.

Requisitions continue. Many people are now lying ill here, suffering from a type of nervous illness, or as it is called, lazaret fever.

The 14th. My brother Joh[ann] Friedrich also fell seriously ill.

Many people are dying now. On the 15th my mother's sister died and on the 19th her husband; both their children, Conrad and his sister, are very ill.

The 19th. I have not removed my clothes for eight days and have not gone to bed because of all the upheaval.

The 30th/31st. It is crawling with Prussians and Russians. They marched through the town all day and all night to go to Braubach, where they were to cross the Rhine.

None of us will forget this year. Whoever has not experienced it personally would not believe the hardship war brings. Thousands dead on the battlefield, thousands crippled, and even more in poverty, misfortune, and misery, thousands who go to an early grave because of this. It is impossible to describe all the misery of war.

This year, everything grew well, especially the potatoes, turnips, and root vegetables.

1814

On New Year's eve, the allies crossed the Rhine.

The 2nd. We had to billet Russian dragoons, an evil type of human from the Turkish border, previously a Turk himself. We have 16 horses in the barn and stables, being fed hay and sheaves of grain; the whole day, even at midnight, food has to be available; whenever two or three have eaten, new people arrive and demand food, and so it goes the whole day; nobody knows which of these passing soldiers are assigned to them. Here, with these [dragoons], we got to know Russians, who have tormented us for the whole month. Oh, if only our posterity will do better than ourselves, who have been betrayed, who have waited so impatiently for those we thought would be our deliverers but turned out to be our devastators. Even if the Russians come as friends and allies to Germany, we should still all take our guns and stop these barbarians. It is better to be dead than tormented.

Many people are dying.

Bovine plague has also broken out, and at the cloister alone 15 animals have already died.

March. All subjects up to the age of 60 had to take up arms, a musket or a lance, and form a Landsturm.

The 25th. The 3rd Nassau regiment and the Landwehr regiment occupied the part of Mainz on the far side of the Rhine, and a sizeable number of townspeople of the nearest posts organized into a Landsturm occupied on this side [of the Rhine] Moss Stream, Biebrich, and the Erbenheim and Hochheim mills. I myself was drawn into the Landwehr regiment on March 2nd, but was fortunately able to leave it very soon.

April. On the 17th there was a victory ceremony [to celebrate Napoleon's abdication], and the whole town was illuminated.

May 1st. On this day the French had to hand over Mainz and all the forts they still held.

The French emperor surrendered himself as a prisoner to the English.

May 15th. Today the Russians marched through, on their way back from France.

On the 21st our livestock was struck by the epidemic; they were brought up to the forest and put in an enclosed copse by the old pond. Four have died and two recovered. I sat with them day and night and gave them one tablespoon [of medicine] in a bottle of water each hour.

June 2nd. Uncountable Russians and Cossacks came through.

The livestock epidemic is spreading rapidly.

The 26th. Huge sums are demanded again for the Landwehr and Jägers that were raised. My mother has to pay another 60 gulden.

July 10th. Grain, with the exception of oats, is cheap. Grain costs 4 gulden 20 kreutzer, wheat 6 gulden 30 kreutzer. Who could have imagined this last winter, with the great masses of people who were trampling the grain with their feet. Everybody was expecting a steep price increase or even famine. Yes, it did cost an unmentionable amount with the masses of people, more than some would like to believe. Nonetheless, we now have a glut. Never before did my mother throw potatoes out onto the compost pile because there were too many; but now it happened. . . . The blessing of God is visible here, yes, the omnipotent hand of God rules everywhere, but most of all, where things seem to be the most hopeless. I don't know how to explain it to myself, how the bakers baked so much bread, how they obtained so much flour. Over the past four months and longer, my mother alone has had to have 15 to 20 loaves baked daily to feed [the soldiers she had to billet].

July 24th. The price of grain is falling constantly.

August 4th. For days we have been taking the cobblestones which we found at the leveled and repaired part of the old stream to our yard. This week we gave these stones to the town to pave the upper Frederick Street. We received 18 gulden per perch, altogether 72 gulden for about 4 perches. This money had to be raised solely by the citizens with carts because now, due to the harvest, they cannot spare their vehicles for the stone-moving forced-labor detail.

The 21st. Boundary-marking stones were placed where the forest bordered fields or meadows.

October 9th. The water of the Kissel Spring is to be channeled into the town, and they are conducting experiments [on how best to do it].

October. In the night of the 10th to 11th, the temperature dropped well below freezing; the grapes are all black.

The 16th and 18th, the feast commemorating the big battle near Leipzig, which took place the previous year, is being celebrated. The Frenchmen left 100,000 dead and injured on the battlefield and had to retreat beyond Hanau and then across the Rhine. In all cities and towns of the allies—the Russians, Austrians, Prussians and all the small monarchies—bonfires were lit on the highest mountains. Near Wiesbaden, on the Bierstadt Mountain, there were three big bonfires, where big tree trunks had been gathered and surrounded by pieces of wood, carpenter's shavings, old oil barrels, and similar things, which produced a fire higher than 50 feet.

October 30th. The whole autumn has been dry, only now did it rain. The crops are coming along nicely, especially the grain. Lying five to six weeks on the dry earth did not harm it.

December. A wolf was spotted in our forested hills, a hunt was organized on the 5th.

The leases and rents of the fields were changed. . . . The princely tax has been raised five times this year. . . .

We are allowed to collect dry wood in the town forest, and we collected several cartloads near Pfaffenborn. On November 1st I cut down two beech trees.

Hay, grain, and potatoes are developing poorly.

Grain prices are rising again. Wheat costs 8 gulden.

The beautiful good horse, which we bought for 13 ½ carolins from a Russian officer on June 5th, had glanders and infected the other horse, which we had bought for 5 gulden (although it was worth more than 100) from a Prussian uhlan on December 1st, 1813. We have almost given up both horses for dead.

During the heavy Russian billeting on January 2nd, we were fortunate to have their dragoons' horses quartered in our stables. Then we got a supply officer with four assistants billeted on us who had to put their horses in the barn [where we store our grain]. If it hadn't been for the supply officer, who was very strict and thrashed them often, everything would have been lost. As it was, we still lost a lot of crops: 90 sheaves of barley were missing, as well as oats and wheat. These Russians were the worst, and through their mistreatment many citizens died, as well as Blum of the lord's mill.

1815

Much construction is going on in upper Frederick Street and in Nero Street.

March. The weather has been relatively mild until now.

On the 8th we sowed summer grass, clover, and hay seeds on the large old stream lot and turned it into a meadow.

The French emperor Napoleon went from the island of Elba back to France; war is expected again.

12th. A big injustice exists in Wiesbaden. An analysis was done of the heavy military billeting which took place last year, and now the whole burden is to be borne by those who own land, the very people who have already suffered most from this burden. They will have to pay a lot, while other rich people, who experienced only light billeting, will get compensation.

The 26th. Today we bought a light carriage.

Mobilization for war against France is beginning.

April 1st. The sheep and their lambs went into the fields. . . .

Starting April 1st we have to supply the local soldiers on a war footing again.

The 18th it froze ice-cold at night.

The 23rd. Postmaster Schlichter is creating a nice garden to the right of the Stumben Gate. He is raising the wall there, and we are supplying the stones. We quarry them at Todthenhohl and receive cartage fees of 3 gulden 30 kreutzer per perch.

May. In the night of the 1st to the 2nd our good spitz dog died, although he wasn't sick.

In upper Frederick Street, near New Alley, close to the house with the stone columns, the book dealer Schellenberg is building a house, and we are carting many sandstones to him from Biebrich.

The 22nd. Today the Nassau soldiers marched off via Schwalbach toward the Netherlands where part of the German army is gathering against the French.

The citizenry is being organized into a Landsturm again.

June 4th. Church Alley is being extended between the Mahre farm and the nunnery's farm through the gardens to Frederick Street.

This year the price of wood is 10 gulden per fathom.

The 18th a big battle took place between the French and Germans near Brussels, where the French were beaten and are retreating.

July 16th. A big victory celebration was held and in the evening the town was lit up.

August 20th. Whoever wants to own a dog has to pay 1 gulden 30 kreutzer annually into the city treasury. The dogs of those who refuse will be eliminated and their owners punished.

September 12th. The owners of the meadows in front of the Diet mill are building a stone weir to water their meadows. For this, I have driven six cartloads full of stones from Sonneberg.

October 1st. Today 400 recruits marched off to the two regiments in Paris.

The 8th. The Russians are returning from France, moving through Mainz to Frankfurt.

The 15th. This week we had marching Russians billeted on us for three days.

The 31st was autumn, there is very little wine.

November 9th. It is beginning to snow and turning very cold.

The 25th/26th we had Hessians marching through during the night.

December 3rd. We had a few unsettled days because of the Prussians moving through on their way home.

There are again wolves in our forested hills. One of them was shot this week and brought into town.

The 17th. Sparrow heads have to be supplied.[19]

December 24th, the 1st Nassau Regiment has returned from France.

This year there was no fruit.

The crops, and really everything else, were mediocre.

There is something special on my mind, seemingly as if a voice had spoken within me: next year there will be something different, but

---

[19] Because sparrows damaged the crops, every inhabitant had to kill fifteen sparrows during the first half of 1816, providing their heads as proof. Those not meeting their quota were charged eight kreutzer per missing head.

something will be missing from the cultivation of the fields, so that not many things will grow in their normal fashion.

1816

January 2nd. Today the cart horses of the local troops who had been in France were auctioned off. We bought the good brown gelding for 170 gulden.

The well in Long Alley near the lower Schützenhof corner was filled in and eliminated.

7th. The weather is very mild. In the upper Frederick Street many new houses are being started.

21st. The Roman bath is to be rebuilt, and work was begun this week. For this, we have carted the necessary timber from Zimmer Place, 72 cartloads, for which we charged 48 kreutzer a load, earning us 57 gulden 30 kreutzer in all. All hedgerows are to be eliminated. The local soldiers still have to be supplied as in wartime. The weather is mild but wet.

February 11th. The weather is now cold. There are huge flocks of wild geese on the fields.

The 23rd. At the moment we are experiencing very light and sunny days. A new school is to be built; plans are being drawn up for that.

March 10th. The wet weather is continuing, and one cannot work in the fields at the moment. The cabbage seedlings, which were still so nice in January, suffered from the cold in February and the wet in March.

The 24th. The new school behind Mill Alley has been started, and all citizens with carts have to transport stones from Sonneberg under compulsory labor. Today the 24th, the old prince died; he was driven to Usingen the night of the 27th.

March. The citizens with carts complained about the heavy burden of compulsory labor. Because of that, the job of furnishing cobblestones and sand for Frederick Street was auctioned off to the lowest bidder for the first time. But as a result, the taxes on property and trades were raised. This was the very first auction of the public carting contract.

The 26th. We fertilized the clover with gypsum. The Thursday oat market is to be supplemented with other crops, and a complete grain market is to be created.

April 3rd. Today April 3rd the cow of local citizen and baker Gottfried Daniel Kron bore a calf in the marketplace which had two complete heads, four eyes and four ears. The heads grew together at the neck, the rest of the body was as with every other calf. But the calf had to be cut out of the cow, though, and soon died. The meat of the cow was distributed among the poor.

April 7th. A mineral spring was discovered between Eppstein and Lorsbach, which is supposed to have been there for 80 years. But because it was directly on the border, the electors of Mainz and Darmstadt had had a big court case about it. During the lawsuit, it was said that the spring had dried up, but it has now welled up again. It is considered to be a miracle because the water is said to heal swiftly all internal and external illnesses. Yes, it is seen as a miracle from God. Many local people are going there, and people from across the forest and across the Rhine also, to collect water.

The 13th the sheep with the lambs stayed in the Perch. We have 17 sheep and seven lambs. I have taken down our old vines, but will replant them soon. The weather is changeable, snow, raw and cold, wet. The 19th it thundered a lot, the night of the 20th it froze solid again. The trees and the hedge are still grey.

The 27th my brother Joh[ann] Heinrich returned from the reserves. . . .

April 27th. The fruit trees are starting to blossom.

May 9th. We bought a big white cow . . . for 10 carolins. It gives 13 liters and one pint of milk.

The famous spring near Lorsbach has already lost its reputation.

The 27th the sheep were shorn. We have sold four of them for 36 gulden. Building work is going on in Frederick and William Streets. The citizens are no longer receiving wood at cost, because this year's timber has been auctioned off at 12 to 15 gulden per fathom to pay for [the town's] many expenses. The weather was changeable, the last few days very wet.

June 4th. I have auctioned the block of oak in Himmelöhr. It was 1 ¾ fathoms, taxed at 5 gulden 35 kreutzer.

Between April 15th and October 15th, no dung can be carted through Sonneberg Gate and William Street.

June 18th. The day of last year's battle of Waterloo was much celebrated. . . .

October 6th. A new barracks is to be built on Frederick Street. . . .

The 13th, two taxes have been raised by the city this year, and two more increases have been proposed. The weather is good for this time of year.

The 20th, the foundations for the barracks are being dug. The snails are causing great damage. They devour entire fields of young corn, something I have never seen before. The price of grain is still increasing. Wheat costs 20 gulden, grain is almost the same. It is beginning to freeze very hard.

The 27th, the cold nights did not harm the snails one bit. The fields are still full of them. People are sowing for the second time.

November 24th. A new forest regulation has been instituted, to the effect that nothing, not even the smallest bit, can be taken from the forest: things like stones, moss, thorns, and other similar things. If people who had lived here 20 years ago were to return now, they would not believe their eyes. It is a sad time for the subjects. A thing, over which we previously had rights, we have had to give up without murmur. Whatever is asked, we have to give. Taxes have been raised eight to ten times. The weather was mild again.

December 1st. The weekly newspaper gave a breakdown of the heavy billeting of 1813 and 1814. It lists the names of those who had too many billetings and those who had too few, what the former received as compensation, and what the latter had to pay. But those who suffered the most from billeting, who remember those days with horror, are listed as having to pay sizeable sums of 80 gulden, 150 gulden, 200 gulden to 1,000 gulden. At that time, it was the custom that every morning everybody had to record in writing the number of people billeted and sign his name to it, and then hand in the form at the billeting office. Many people did not fill out forms, many could not write anything down because of sickness or other disturbances. Even in the houses of respectable citizens, there were so many people [billeted], that they did not know how many there were and which ones were their soldiers. This was even the case with us; there were 15 men sitting down [to eat], then soon after others came and demanded food too, and after these still others, and so it went the whole day. How could we keep track of the 24 to 28 men who were permanently billeted on us, especially when they were moved from one house to another. And if there were 50 to 80 men billeted in a house, its owners were no longer in charge at all, but had to take things as they came. In the end there were no more plates, spoons, or forks left in the house. The house was open, soldiers came and went as they pleased, especially the Russians. Other people took their forms every morning to the billeting office, but instead of listing the eight or 10 men they had actually billeted, wrote down 12 or 14. These swindlers are now to receive compensation from those who were lucky to hang onto their houses, fields, and, most of all, their lives. The civil servants who had officers quartered with them are now to receive full compensation for it, as if they did not have to shoulder the burdens of war. Because I was healthy then and remained healthy, every morning I was able to hand in our forms with the right number of people indicated. Thus, in the final analysis, we came out even.

10

JULIE PELLIZZONE

Journal

1813–1815

Jeanne-Julie Pellizzone (1768–1837) was a well-off woman from the port city of Marseille. Her father, Etienne Moulinneuf, was a noted local artist and official painter of the city. He helped create its Academy of Sculpture and Painting. A progressive man of the Enlightenment, he believed in women's education and personally supervised that of his daughter. She was exceptionally well educated for a woman of her time. In 1783 Julie married Joseph-Vincent Pellizzone, a merchant who later became a military administrator in 1792. He was absent for long periods, and Julie rarely visited him. On his return to Marseille in 1801, he began living openly with a mistress. Julie retaliated by installing a lover of her own, the painter Girardon, in her apartment at the corner of the Cours Belsunce and Canebière, major streets in the city. From her window, she could literally see the events she describes in her journal. Julie's public liaison with Girardon, morally unacceptable for a woman, led to her social marginalization. In 1811 she started to keep a journal. A political chronicle, rather than an intimate diary, Julie's journal shows life in Marseille during the Hundred Days, the White Terror, and foreign occupation—a time of great turmoil and confusion that accompanied the end of the Napoleonic Wars. She offers not only what she witnessed, but also her sense of others' perceptions of these events, including those of the soldiers. It is also one of the few accounts of the period written by a woman.

Julie Pellizzone, *Souvenirs, 1787–1815* (Indigo/Coté-femmes/Publications de l'Université de Provence, n.d., n.p.), 1:275–369; and Julie Pellizzone, *Souvenirs: Journal d'une Marseillaise, 1815–1824* (Indigo/Coté-femmes/Publications de l'Université de Provence, 2001, n.p.), 2:21–108.

February–May 1813

The middle of February 1813 was marked by a host of circumstances disagreeable to the citizens of Marseille. First, there was despair in the families of young men forced to leave for the army, 350,000 in all, to replace those who perished miserably in Russia. Then an extraordinary tax was decreed by the prefect to recruit 60 armed cavalrymen to replace those who died of cold in Russia. A collection was started to raise the money, but since no one contributed, three classes of taxes were established; the first for 800 francs, the second 350, and the last 100, to be paid within 24 hours by the city's businessmen and merchants. . . .

Then, the same week, a decree on bakers was proclaimed that suppressed all wholesale bread dealers; in consequence, many people were without bread.

Saturday, February 20, at 8 a.m., several carts of superb English merchandise were led to La Plaine[1] to be burned by government order, which was carried out. The operation lasted until 5 p.m. In the middle of La Plaine, a great fire was lit and the many stevedores, hired for this, did nothing all day but throw into the flames muslin, percales, nankeen, shawls, lace, air-spun cotton, etc., as well as great quantities of trinkets they thoroughly smashed before casting in. What the fire did not consume was carefully gathered and thrown into the sea. When it was over, La Plaine looked like a mountain of ash that made you shiver when you thought of where it came from and imagined how many French people have nothing to cover themselves with. . . .

April–May 1813

Yesterday night, May 3, 1813, around 6 p.m., the English frigate blockading the port audaciously came up, cut the cable of an anchored ship, and captured it. It then crossed in front of the port entrance and, despite the battery fire of Forts St. Jean and St. Nicholas, fired several cannonades and launched a few firepots at the port, to set it ablaze. . . .

The forts' cannons fired on the frigate nonstop, but without harming it although it was well within range. The women of the Catalans,[2] who saw cannonballs falling like hail around them, fled with their children and most precious belongings, and sought shelter in the city, whose inhabitants gathered on the heights to see this extraordinary spectacle, because an enemy vessel had never before come so close.

[1] A military parade ground.
[2] A suburb near the port.

July 1813

On July 6, 1813, the young men of the department's honor guard dined at Prefect Thibaudeau's,[3] where they had music, salvos, etc. The next morning they left for Lyon[4] to be organized. The prefect, General Dumuy, and other high-ranking officers accompanied them. . . . They are mounted, dressed as hussars. All the young men of good family have paid for their own equipment and left for the active army, hoping to become officers after one year's service in the emperor's honor guard. When they were reviewed here, there was one who didn't know how to mount his horse. . . .

August 1813

Today, August 11, 1813, around 10 a.m., a courier arrived followed by a six-horse carriage. We figured that it was the announcement of peace, which has been rumored for some time. This news gained credit to the point that the market women of the Cours began to cry, sing, dance, and kiss each other, etc. At that moment, the cart loaded with the wood necessary to construct the grandstands for the fireworks display having arrived, they redoubled their cries and applause. . . . Please God that this news is not unfounded and that peace, so greatly desired, finally arrives! They say it will be announced at the St. Napoleon Day's festival. That's on Sunday; we won't have long to wait.

The St. Napoleon took place without peace being announced. It was a rumor started by a letter of Mr. Pedelupé, actor, written from Paris to his father who has long been established in Marseille as a turner. They say that he has been questioned by the police about this letter, which he showed everywhere and which said that a treaty had been signed. . . .

The English are still up to their tricks. They entered Cassis[5] the other night, after capturing the convoy anchored in the port. They took the merchandise that had been offloaded into storehouses, burned a few houses, etc. Finally, they reembarked, but they say that Cassis is surrounded and that no one can leave, because plague is feared. The inhabitants are being forced to undergo a quarantine of sorts.

February 1814

The 1814 Carnival was very sad at Marseille. The invasion of Russian, Prussian, and Austrian troops, etc., has caused great consternation. Balls were forbidden; yet, out of consideration for the victories they say

---

[3] A former revolutionary politician who served as prefect of the department of the Bouches-du-Rhône under Napoleon.
[4] A city several hundred miles north of Marseille.
[5] A coastal village near Marseille.

Emperor Napoleon has won, they permitted the Grand Theater to hold on Fat Thursday a Venetian-type ball, which ended at 11 p.m. And, Fat Sunday, a nocturnal ball was given; Monday a Venetian ball, and Tuesday a nocturnal ball; all cost 25 sols[6] per person; this is unheard of and shows the misery of the times.

These balls were probably very poorly composed, because upstanding people have no desire to dance at this moment; everyone is worried about their fortune, their children. . . . Taxes are rising sharply; they are doubled and redoubled periodically; orders to leave for the army circulate with profusion. The billeting of soldiers crushes the citizen, because we are obliged to put them up every week, for several days at a time, costing each household 4 or 5 francs each week. We have suffered every sort of vexation and this at a moment when everybody is ruined. All this is well suited to extinguish all desire to dance or put on a mask.

On top of all this, it is excessively cold, and Ash Wednesday, on the morning of February 23, the ground was covered with snow (something extraordinary in the city). It continued to fall all day long without interruption. . . .

March 1814

Marseille is currently in a singular position. News of the fall of Lyon, taken by the enemies (they say) on March 21, 1814, inspires great agitation. Everyone is full of all sorts of hopes and fears, and everyone starts or spreads rumors according to the sentiment that animates them. Most likely, we will soon be visited by the English, just like the inhabitants of Bordeaux. . . . Livorno is also in their power, and the season is beginning to favor a landing. On the other hand, some of the troops that took Lyon are marching south, but General Augereau is defending this flank, and it is assumed that Eugène, viceroy of Italy, has just reinforced him to oppose the progress of the enemy toward us. This is good, because the inhabitants cannot be counted upon to defend themselves zealously.

Despite the orders and proclamations of Masséna and Admiral Ganteaume,[7] there is much apathy in this region. The young men are either with the army or have already perished in the debacles of Russia and Germany. Their fathers don't want to fight, so it is difficult to get them to take up arms. I don't know how it will all turn out, but we are in a terrible crisis. Everything is up in the air; we go to bed each evening not knowing if the night will be calm.

---

[6] A worker earned about twenty sols daily.

[7] Duke of Rivoli, André Masséna was one of Napoleon's marshals. In 1814, he was military commander of southeastern France. Count Honoré Ganteaume served as a special mobilization commissioner in southern France.

Yesterday night, March 28, all the soldiers were assembled, the outposts reinforced, etc. Toulon,[8] above all, is greatly threatened, and many of its inhabitants have retreated here hoping for greater safety. Until now, Marseille has viewed the theater of war from afar; may it never be the scene of combat! Many people who found themselves in Lyon on March 21 have come here under enemy passports. It is said they had to promise not to take up arms against the invaders.

April 1814

On April 8th, Good Friday, Prefect Thibaudeau put up posters announcing the fall of Paris; the enemies entered it on March 30. This news provoked a singular sensation in Marseille. At the corner of the Canebière, where the first poster was placed, a large crowd formed, and there was an extraordinary hubbub. Some people are aggrieved by this news, while others rejoice. I dare say the latter outnumber the former. . . .

The 4th of this month, the arrival of a large number of wounded soldiers from Lyon was announced, along with an invitation to the people of Marseille to furnish sheets, old clothing, mattresses, etc. They were even going to billet them on the bourgeois, but the difficulty of having doctors and surgeons care for them, thus dispersed, scuttled the plan. They are expected today, April 8. So many victims!!!!!!

The wounded only arrived on April 10, Easter Day, around 12:30. There were ten heavily loaded carts. They were put in the General Hospital. To make room, other wounded, who were there before, were transferred to the Lazaret.[9]

April 14 and 15, 1814

Since morning, a rumor, which few believe, has been circulating in town: The Senate has convened in Paris, declared Buonaparte[10] stripped of his empire, and proclaimed Louis XVIII legitimate king of the French; that Buonaparte will be relegated to the Isle of Elba, where he will be decently treated on the condition that he leave the universe in peace.

This rumor required confirmation, and everyone was doubtful. But, around 2 p.m., lots of people headed for the Aix Gate. Around 3 p.m., it began to be said that a courier was coming, bearing this news. People cited Monsieur Albertas the younger, who had just arrived with an olive branch in his hat and who had overtaken the courier. Soon, the whole

---

[8] France's main Mediterranean naval base, about fifty miles east of Marseille.

[9] The building used to quarantine those arriving at Marseille by sea.

[10] Like most royalist opponents of Napoleon, Pellizzone used this spelling of Napoleon's name to highlight his foreign (Corsican) origins, delegitimize his rule, and cast him as a usurper.

city was on the road to Aix, cries of joy were heard, people ran in mass in the same direction; it looked like ocean waves in a raging storm. The surge grew until 6 p.m., when this blessed courier finally arrived with great difficulty in the city, for the crowd was so considerable. . . .

How to describe the enthusiasm of the people in Aix Street and on the Cours! All the upstanding folk of Marseille in the crowd had decorated their hats with white paper cockades,[11] since they lacked any other kind, and waved white handkerchiefs like flags. Cries to the heavens of "Long Live the King!" resonated in the hearts of all true French people. . . . No, the revolution never offered anything like it! Someone took from his pocket a coin with the king's effigy on it, to show it to someone; a crowd threw itself at him to kiss it. Poor French! You have suffered so much, be happy now and right your wrongs as much as possible.

Finally, with mounting excitement, the people, truly sovereign at this moment, carried itself in a fury to Prefect Thibaudeau, notorious for having signed the death sentence of Louis XVI. Luckily, he was not home. The guard box at his door was smashed, but they respected all the other authorities. From there, they went to the Buonaparte Column, a nimble sailor scaled it and put a rope around the neck of the bust of the tyrant. It was pulled down. The rope was very long. About 2,000 men harnessed themselves to it and dragged it through all the city's gutters.

A furious crowd followed this cortege, armed with the debris of the guard box, delivering great blows to the face of this enemy of the human race. What an example, great God, for evildoers who prefer to dominate through fear rather than by love! This man, who still yesterday made the whole world tremble, is today in the mud!!! His head, separated from his body, was finally dragged to Portogallo[12] by children. . . .

The promenade that bore his odious name was ravaged from top to bottom, and the debris . . . used to construct bonfires. Soon there were bonfires across the city, before almost every house. Windows were illuminated spontaneously, and with all the more joy since this had never been ordered under the tyrant's reign. Thibaudeau's servants carried to the nearest bonfire the seat on which he customarily sat, and the people were happy to burn it! . . .

Everyone's hat has a white cockade, men and women. No one slept the first night. But it must be said, in praise of the city guard, that it greatly contributed to maintaining good order and that, in the first moment when the people threw off the yoke, all the bourgeois that composed it

[11] Insignia worn on hats.
[12] One of the city gates.

assembled in arms and conducted continual patrols all night long and all the next day, April 15. That day, the prisoners in the Hall of Justice . . . were freed with much clamor. They wanted to free those in the Château d'If,[13] but the commander refused until he had received orders. A 21-gun salute was fired on the quay and another on the Cours in honor of Louis XVIII. Long Live the King!

It is said that when the bust of Buonaparte, dragged in the mud, passed before a butcher's shop, the proprietor dumped a pan of blood over his face saying, "There, you love blood so much, drink that!"

March 1815

For Marseille, March 4, 1815, was a day that will be remembered forever (it was a Saturday). Already the previous evening, the rumor spread that Buonaparte had left Elba and landed at Gulf Juan, near Cannes, with a troop of 800 men as determined as himself. Having become public, the news caused an extreme uproar in the city. The people went in a crowd to Masséna's house, who promised from his balcony to take all necessary measures against such an unexpected event. In effect, he immediately left for Toulon to prepare the city's defenses and march troops against the common enemy.

The urban guard suddenly assembled and, without waiting for orders, two registers were opened to indicate those who wanted to go off to fight and those who could not leave their homes: everybody signed up to leave. That night, the artillerymen assembled around a bust of Louis XVIII and paraded by torchlight to the sound of drums and music for part of the night, accompanied by the usual enthusiasm and cries of "Long Live the King." . . . But, despite these patriotic expressions, everyone regretted the unpardonable imprudence of our government for not having removed from the face of the earth this extremely dangerous individual, who caused the death of so many thousands of men and who is perhaps going to burden us again with incalculable ills! . . .

He stayed calmly on Elba during the cold season, but no sooner had the breath of spring begun to be felt than he set off. He has arrived, and already terror and consternation are among us. . . . He landed March 2nd at Gulf Juan. They say he spent the night sleeping on the shore with his little troop: that the next day, they went to Antibes and, having arrived, sent a detachment of 25 men with two officers to enter the city. They arrived crying, "Long Live Napoleon. Long Live the Emperor." Antibes is a fortified town, and the loyal garrison lifted the drawbridge

---

[13] An island fortress guarding the approaches to the port.

and took the 27 men prisoner. . . . Buonaparte then continued on his way with the rest of his troop. Some say that he is heading for the mountains of Piedmont to go into Italy, others say that he is marching toward Grenoble and from there to Lyon where, they say, he has many supporters. . . . And that is exactly what makes me tremble, that he still has many partisans, mainly in Northern France, not to mention that the entire army is still for him, despite the unexpected benefits the officers received from our excessively generous monarch. . . .

Sunday March 5 was a day of consternation for the city. Everybody gathered and asked each other about the event. Everyone made up his own story and everyone agreed that this was going to cause us new misfortunes. . . . Above all Marseille, which rallied to the Bourbons[14] so enthusiastically, what will happen to her if Buonaparte wins? Already they say that he said that, when he takes the reins of government, the first thing he will do will be to raze Marseille. . . .

That night at 11 p.m., the troops sent from Toulon by General Masséna arrived at Marseille. They made the entire march in one day. . . . They were welcomed with a bust of the king and cries of "Long Live Henri IV"[15] and "Long Live the King." But that didn't produce much of an effect. These soldiers never once unlocked their jaws to join their voices to ours! . . . However, they had but little time to refresh themselves and rest, because they left for Aix at 5 a.m. . . . It seems that the ill is pressing, since so much haste is being made to remedy it, but it would have been so much easier to prevent it! . . .

Monday March 6 at 5 a.m., the members of the urban or royal guard designated to set off received the order to assemble . . . at 9 a.m. with arms and baggage. . . .

Tuesday night, March 7th, a troop of urban guardsmen, having dined with the regular army officers, left the inn drunk, singing "Long Live Henri IV" and crying "Long Live the King." The people gathered around them. When they came to the Canebière, they were all taken by the hand and made to dance. The market women were mixed with them, and everybody thought that there was good news. In an instant, the rumor spread that the tiger had been caught. The whole city soon assembled on the Cours. Everyone was singing, crying, embracing, thanking each other, but this effusion of joy was short. . . .

Wednesday the 8th, no news, general consternation. Thursday the 9th, St. Françoise Day, the effervescence was at a fever pitch. From the

---

[14] The royal family of France until the Revolution.
[15] A popular king who ruled France in the early seventeenth century.

morning on, the rumor spread that Buonaparte was trapped in a village near Grenoble called St. Bonnet. People gathered everywhere, because they thought that this news was going to be announced. Effectively, a proclamation was posted by Masséna, in which he described the measures he had taken against the common enemy, who was marching with striking audacity and rapidity toward Grenoble and Lyon, where he hoped to find a party in his favor, and from there march in force on Paris, where he claimed that he would be on the 20th of this month in order to celebrate the birthday of the king of Rome, his son.

When they realized that the proclamation did not say he was trapped, everybody dispersed and the day was pretty calm. But around 9 p.m., when least expected, a cry was heard all around: "He has been taken! He is caught!" Nothing but this was heard in the streets and nothing was seen but people running until they were out of breath to carry this news to their friends. . . . In an instant the city was afoot, just like the day of the arrival of the courier bringing word of peace. The cries, songs, hugs from strangers, fireworks on every corner, at every door. Those who had nothing else to burn, burnt commodes, armoires; everyone did his best to express his joy! . . . What caused this general rejoicing was a letter from Mr. Suchay of Aix, who wrote to Mr. Moutte of Marseille that Buonaparte had been caught, that he was trapped at St. Bonnet, and that General Bertrand, his worthy companion of adventures, had turned him over himself to the French. A crowd went to General Masséna's to know if he had received word. He said that, no, he still didn't know anything for certain, so that this news, not being official, needed confirmation. Thus, the enthusiasm of the Marseillais cooled down a bit. . . . The dancing stopped, and around 11 p.m. everybody went back home.

The next day, Friday, the city seemed deserted. A great letdown had followed the hot fever of the night before. No one was seen in the streets. . . .

The fishwives received in each market a different anonymous letter in which they were blamed for always being the first to cry "Long Live the King" and sing songs against Buonaparte. They were threatened that, once he triumphed, he would wash his hands in their blood. This warning weakened their ardor a bit. The messenger who delivered these letters was imprisoned, but he did not know who had given him the commission.

Yesterday, a poster was pasted up announcing that, on the 9th, Buonaparte had been repulsed before Grenoble. Today, Sunday March 12th, another appeared, officially declaring that Buonaparte had entered Grenoble the 7th and that disloyalty had delivered it to him. . . .

I can't express the effect this news had on the city. All the men gathered together crying "To arms, to arms, women, children arm yourselves!" This cry was hair-raising! . . . In effect, several women were ready to march off to follow their husbands or sons, or to go help those who had gone before. . . . A crowd went off to Masséna's to demand arms. He appeared on the balcony to ask the people to remain calm, assuring them that there were more than enough [soldiers] to contain the enemy. At this, everyone left, very discontent, and panic spread. Some said that Masséna is betraying us, that he delayed the departure of the urban guard as long as he could to give the enemy time to reach his objective. . . . Others find that he acted very prudently to not give arms to people who, under the pretext of following our avengers, might use them to vex and pillage us.

Everyone theorizes, discusses, and sighs: Everyone tells a story, true or false. One tells you that the city is full of proclamations spread by Buonaparte's agents, promising a general pardon to everybody, except two generals, Augereau and Marmont, who betrayed him. . . . Another assures you that if Buonaparte wins, Marseille will be razed from top to bottom for all of the blows it has struck against him. . . . The women cry and the men are hardly more reassured. . . . Since the revolution, I have not seen such a sad day as this.

However, the Count d'Artois[16] is at Lyon with loyal troops, and his presence will doubtless keep the Lyonnais in line. That is our last hope; but there will still be bloodshed, since the surrender of Grenoble furnished important forces to the enemy. It would have been so easy to arrest and destroy him before he arrived there! . . . But no one wanted to. He was welcomed everywhere, everywhere they let him pass. . . . O French, French, do you want to be dishonored forever? . . .

Monday March 13th was as sad as Sunday; the news gets worse and worse. They say that Buonaparte was welcomed by Lyon, and that the Count d'Artois had to leave in haste with a few officers personally devoted to him. . . . Our last hope is in Paris, where Louis XVIII has joined his brother. . . . The Holy Sacrament is displayed in every church, and the prayer of 40 hours is ordered for the king's safety. . . . But we need more than prayers.

They say that the urban guard will return since, not having been able to catch Buonaparte, it serves no purpose where it is, but might be very

---

[16]Younger brother of Louis XVI and Louis XVIII. He was crowned King Charles X of France in 1824 and ruled until overthrown in the revolution of 1830.

useful here, where there is terrible unrest and gatherings very dangerous to public tranquility. . . . One suspects there is treason in everything happening here, and the people might well take extreme measures. . . . Masséna has brought more troops from Toulon to contain the people . . . but it is precisely the sight of soldiers that irritates them, knowing that they have Buonaparte in their hearts. . . .

Thursday, March 16, 1814, the Prince d'Angoulême, husband of our august princess and son of the Count d'Artois, arrived at Marseille at 4:30 p.m. The regular army troops and what remains of the urban guard went to meet him along with the authorities. . . . But what a difference between this reception and that which we gave his father several months ago! In this sad moment, there are neither celebrations nor triumphal arches. He comes to ask for the fidelity and aid of his subjects, and when [the mayor] gave his speech at the Aix Gate, everyone cried, even the prince.

However, the whole city came to welcome him. The cries of "Long Live the King, Long Live d'Angoulême" sounded all around. The white flag fluttered everywhere, and if the line troops hadn't been suspect, there would have been much hope. The prince entered the city on horseback, preceded by the cavalry of the urban guard and gendarmes, with Masséna at his side. When he came to the middle of the Cours, a loud voice shouted out, "Prince, you are poorly escorted." He continued his route, greeting everyone with that natural ease, that affability common to all the Bourbons, above all his father the Count d'Artois, whom he greatly resembles. He lodged at the prefecture where he dined and then, at the demand of the people who burned to see him, went to the theater where the crowd rushed enthusiastically. Those unable to enter contented themselves with running around the city in groups singing "Long Live Henri IV" and "My God, My King, My Dame." All the streets through which he passed on his way to the theater were illuminated somewhat, but the rest of the city remained dark and empty, as is appropriate at this moment.

The prince left Friday the 17th, at 5 a.m., to go to Toulon and assess its condition. . . .

The free companies are being organized energetically. They are going to march to the Nîmes camp under the orders of the Duke d'Angoulême. . . . The desire to join up is great, but it is not only love of the king that motivates the men. It is that most, having neither work nor fortune, see in the military a resource. Where will the money be found to pay them? Treasures are needed, but where to find them? . . .

Tuesday the 21st, the free companies march in great crowds to Nîmes, but no news of Napoleon. That night, there was a large gathering . . . to see a small transport ship from Naples, full of men devoted to Buonaparte, which was allowed in all the way to the end of the quay, I don't know why. These people started shouting "Long Live the Emperor" on board the ship and everybody gathered to hear them. . . . The urban guard went there too and asked why they were shouting. They responded that they thought Napoleon had regained the throne and that it was for that reason they were shouting. One of them added that Marie-Louise, his wife, was coming with 30,000 men to support his cause. This individual was put in prison, but the others were left free, I don't know why. News of the arrival of Marie-Louise on our shores with an army spread new terror in our hearts.

The 24th and 25th, nothing new: false rumors, some good, some bad; nothing positive. This uncertainty is cruel. We don't know where Buonaparte is, and such an active man doesn't just sit around doing nothing. The Parisians are favorably inclined toward the king. On the 16th there was a royal session, whose details are extremely touching. The king said that he did not fear death, but that he was afraid for France. Everybody cried and swore to die for him. . . . But his enemy's army grows each day, thanks to traitors who join him. And those are Frenchmen! Oh eternal shame! Those are Frenchmen who tear apart the fatherland and abandon their king to follow a Corsican. . . .

April 1815

On Sunday night [April 2nd], the alarm was raised because of squabbling between the regular army troops and bourgeois. The rumor spread that the urban guard wanted to disarm the line troops and that the line troops had resolved to disarm the guard. However, nothing happened but several spats between individuals.

Monday, April 3rd, the festival of the Annunciation, which came in Holy Week, was celebrated. The good news was confirmed. Enthusiasm was rekindled and the free companies were able to recruit. On Tuesday the 4th, the market women and fishwives collected donations that they used to corrupt the soldiers of the line troops, so that a large number deserted in order to transfer into the free companies. The line officers are not happy about that. . . .

Wednesday, April 5th, organization of the first cohort of the 2nd legion of the national guard. . . . Crowds of soldiers pass to the royal flags, deserting those of their officers, correctly suspected of being part of Buonaparte's conspiracy. That same night, the alarm was raised because of these gentlemen. . . . The entire urban guard was in arms the whole night, because the women, having learned that the line troops had received orders to go to Toulon, had plotted to surround them and make them desert or take away their arms. . . .

Monday, April 10th, the bad news is confirmed. The Duke d'Angoulême has been beaten and defeated. Some say he was taken prisoner; others, that he fled by ship. The enemy is marching on us unopposed, and we are between a rock and a hard place. . . .

The urban guard was summoned to an extraordinary assembly . . . and were given an order that prevents them from being permanently under arms and tells them to obey calmly and confidently the orders they will be given. It is assumed that they are going to be ordered to don Napoleon's cockade, or that they are going to be disarmed in order to leave the city in the hands of Masséna's troops, and God knows what will happen then! Others say that the Duke d'Angoulême surrendered and that he obtained permission to sail away from Sète[17] on condition that Marseille and Toulon submit to Napoleon. One can imagine the consternation reigning in the city. The people are enraged, the guard is harassed and despairing. However, the officers of the line troops are arriving from Toulon and shout "Long Live the Emperor." The people want to massacre them, but the urban guard prevents it. . . .

[April 12th] The tricolor flag flies over public buildings, the tricolor cockade adorns the line officers' hats, which is an effrontery, a kind of arrogance that nothing else equals. The people are upset, the white flags have disappeared, the lilies[18] have been hidden, and new-style posters proclaim the return of the "emperor." . . .

April 13th was very stormy. Greatly agitated, the people circulated in groups in the streets, and the multitude, having approached the town hall, overcame the guard and pulled down the tricolor flag. After this, they fell upon the small number of those with the same kind of cockade, and the urban guard had great difficulty saving them from the popular fury. There were two who wanted to cry "Long Live the Emperor." The women assailed them with blows from chairs and would have beaten them senseless if they had been allowed. All that took place to repeated cries of "Long Live the King," and many men have taken up the white cockade again. The calm folk are upset by this tumult, because they think it will be used as a pretext to send troops here, although Masséna promised not to as long as the city submitted gracefully. . . .

---

[17] A port west of Marseille.
[18] Symbol of the Bourbons, as was the color white in general.

At noon the 15th, the first of the line troops sent by Masséna arrived. They consisted of about 30 or 40 men. They had the arrogance to arrive with laurel branches in their shakos. The crowd gathered round them, booing and yelling at the top of their lungs, "Long Live the King," and, without the urban guard, their cheek would have cost them dearly. The main body of troops arrived next, 700 to 800 strong, but without laurels and most even without cockades. The urban guard [which] had gone to meet them, preceded them and also closed up the line of march to contain the people. All stores were closed, and the terror was general. However, everything was calm. No one cried either "Long Live the King" or "Long Live the Emperor." Both sides kept silent, and everybody was well-behaved, something quite extraordinary in such a circumstance.

All the essential posts that had been occupied by the urban guard have been filled by line troops, so that the urban guard has been stripped of part of its functions. The city seems deserted and consternation reigns everywhere. They say that General Grouchy is at Aix with a considerable body of troops and that he is marching on us at Buonaparte's orders. . . . We are told that he wants to humiliate us and that he will force us to wear the cockade and display tricolor flags; that he also wants to avenge the emperor for all the outrages the city of Marseille has committed against him. He'll have a hard time punishing all of the guilty.

Effectively, the same day, April 15th, as night was falling, the troop I mentioned entered Marseille. They numbered 1,500 to 1,800 men, led by a band and not escorted by the urban guard as had happened that morning. The populace gathered around that troop, crying "Long Live the King." They were accompanied in this way all along Aix Street down to the Cours. When it arrived there, the troop stopped and deployed in battle order. They loaded their weapons in full view of the people, who did not stop shouting. But finally the troop moved off to the sound of drums, crying "Long Live the Emperor, Down with the Bourbons, Down with the Lilies, Shit on the Urban Guard." The officers were like lunatics, making their soldiers cry out and turning them against the people. This moment was terrible, above all at the hour it happened: It was almost night and despite the horror inspired by this horde of cannibals, unworthy of being called French, cries of "Long Live the King" still answered the vociferations of those madmen. An unfortunate young man who fell into their hands was dragged off with them; what did they do with him? . . .

Today, April 16th, everything seemed tranquil. The avant-garde of the cavalry we expected arrived very calmly at 10 a.m. . . . The cavalry arrived after noon, numbering 200 from different corps, with nothing French about them, neither faces, clothes, nor character. They seem like Cossacks or barbarians or, more accurately, bandits, and they are conducting themselves in the heart of their fatherland as if it were a conquered land. They are being lodged and fed by the bourgeois, and they permit themselves to mistreat them and lay down the law. But all the bourgeois are not in a mood to endure it, and we will be very lucky if there is no incident.

Yesterday night, April 16th, the infantry officers gathered together, arm in arm, and, having left the cabaret, ran through the city shouting abominable songs against the king and the Duke d'Angoulême. . . . This racket lasted all night with horrible cries and vociferations, without their leaders doing anything to stop it. . . .

In the night of April 18th to 19th, some of the regular army troops from Aix left; and during the same day, the 19th, others arrived from Aix to take their place. They came at noon without raising a ruckus or shouting like the others. But that night, an abominable crisis occurred. . . . More than 100 officers of the different infantry and cavalry regiments here assembled to drink at Château-Vert, at Arenc.[19] They went there by coach and, from that point, the upstanding people were warned that there would be trouble upon their return. In effect, these gentlemen came back drunk; and to consummate their intoxication, went to drink liquor at the bottom of the Canebière. . . . When completely drunk, they began their infernal vociferations and cries of "Long Live the Emperor." Several imprudent bourgeois responded with "Long Live the King." At this, these lunatics drew their sabers and attacked. Everyone fled, and cries of fear and horror replaced those of [political] opinion. . . . The stevedores at Cul-de-Boeuf grabbed bars and came in mass to attack the officers. Fortunately, a hastily assembled patrol of the urban guard halted and dissuaded them; because, if they had carried out their plan, there would have been abominable carnage. . . .

The cavalrymen, the sort of Cossacks I have already described, who are lodged and fed by the bourgeois at 5 francs per day and who breathe only murder and pillage, noisily assembled, armed with sabers, carbines, pistols, uttering threats and horrible curses, shouting to the people: "Beat it, scum!" They took their horses and went together to the Cours, the Canebière, and the neighboring streets. . . . At the same time, the general alarm was sounded everywhere. The cry "To Arms" was

[19] A building used for festive gatherings.

heard on all sides, and the urban guard assembled as fast as possible to try to prevent even worse misfortunes.

All this was very frightening and would have doubtless finished catastrophically if Monsieur Raymond, the provisional mayor of Marseille, hadn't had the good sense to place himself at the head of a patrol and tell the commander of the cavalry in question that the conduct of his troops was very imprudent and that it could cause the greatest misfortunes by exasperating the people. He concluded by telling him that he held him responsible for whatever happened. This threat calmed the fury of these barbarians a bit, and, the urban guard having quickly mobilized, calm was reestablished. But what a horrible night, where murder and pillage were only avoided by luck. . . .

The next day, April 20th, it rained, which calmed spirits a bit. . . .

The morning of the 21st, our French barbarians left the city, regretting not having been able to pillage it. And we watched them leave with the regret of not having hung them from the gallows. . . .

General Brune has come to replace Masséna at Marseille. He ordered a general review of the national guard and line troops for Thursday, April 27th. This measure displeased everyone and is very impolitic, because putting the urban guard face-to-face with the regular army troops is putting enemies before each other. And, moreover, the people who will gather in crowds [to watch] might commit some rash act that will force these gentlemen to come to blows. Thus, everything possible was done to convince the general to abandon this plan and hold the two reviews separately, but without success. He is too attached to the idea of being able to write to his emperor that he made the national guard fraternize with the line troops, and this consideration trumped all others.

The night of the 26th, there was a fight in Aix Street between the soldiers barracked at the Infirmes[20] and inhabitants of the neighborhood. The first cried "Long Live the Emperor," the others "Long Live the King." The soldiers drew their sabers, something they readily do, and a poor devil who was going home peacefully received a saber blow on the thigh, from which he died the next day. He was a 64-year-old man, father of seven children. The urban guard stopped the tumult and saved the life of the soldiers, on whom the murder of this poor man would have been avenged. . . .

General Brune arrived at 3 p.m. [on April 27th] . . . escorted by gendarmes. He reviewed the national guard and line troops. He then had the staff of the national guard gather round him, and he made a much

---

[20] A former hospital.

more respectful speech than the other day, but no less banal. . . . Afterward, he saluted everybody and everyone left in silence. The urban guard marched off first. When it had left, the line troop had a good time yelling "Long Live the Emperor." Several spectators responded "Long Live the King," but without consequence. . . .

Nothing is more singular than the present situation of Marseille. Buonaparte's government is up and running, but royalism is the sole dominant sentiment. Rich and poor alike have only one opinion: It is for the king. The line troops form a world unto themselves. Nonetheless, there are among the soldiers many royalists, as well as others, in even greater number, who are just machines who can be made to move at will. The officers, however, are all the same, all completely infected. . . . Every day there is some brawl between the soldiers and the people, who allow themselves to boo the soldiers as soon as they open their mouths to cry "Long Live the Emperor!" . . .

May 1815

On Sunday morning, May 21st, Marseille was placed under martial law; here we are, entirely at the discretion of the soldiers. . . .

Soldiers are being billeted everywhere to collect taxes; they refuse to receive IOUs and demand exorbitant sums. In addition, incendiary posters have been placed at every corner, denouncing those who fought for the king; and in every street, the soldiers insult and spit upon those who displease them. . . .

There has never been a night as frightful as the 25th. All these [officers] returning from parade, assembled in St. Ferréol Street; and there, they began their uproar, their cries, their threats, etc. Soon the people began to flee in all directions, away from that troop of cannibals with naked swords or sabers in hand and running after the people to make them shout "Long Live the Emperor." An instant later, gunshots were fired on the Canebière. And thus began the dance. . . . The night that followed made it all the more terrible. We heard the clash of arms, shouts of rage, cries of fright, the footfalls of those who were running to escape the furor of their pursuers, and all that was horrible. . . . The commanders did nothing to stop it. And the tumult only calmed down around 11 p.m., when the officers tired of pursuing, sabering, etc., and when they found no one left to address. . . . If these people are paid to make the government odious and unbearable, they are doing a fine job, and Buonaparte is greatly obliged to them.

The morning of the 26th, we were suddenly awakened by a great noise of cannon fire, and I thought it was a continuation of last night's scene. . . . But not at all. It was the festival of the Champ de Mai.[21] . . . The bust of Buonaparte was led around the city, carried and escorted by line officers, led by musicians, playing and singing songs similar to those of the Terror. . . . The officers finally went off to dine. And, during that time, the soldiers had fun throwing down and breaking all shop signs that did not bear the word "Imperial." The Canebière and the Cours were inundated with soldiers engaged in this operation, climbing up to the second floor of houses to detach the signs. The inhabitants, who had carefully shut themselves inside, had the satisfaction of hearing their facades demolished so that the signs could be undone and then thrown to the ground with cries of "Long Live the Emperor." . . .

But while some were thus occupied, more active ones, who had gone to drink, were told that a gardener in the neighborhood had written on his wall "Long Live the King." They went off to find him. The poor man was working in his garden. They asked him if he had written those words on the wall. He answered that, unable to either read or write, it could not have been him. They ordered him to erase it and, upon his refusal, slit his stomach with a saber blow. The unfortunate man fell, and his entrails spilled out beside him. Then these brave men entered the garden, took all the money they found, destroyed the garden, grabbed pitchforks, bars, and other instruments of carnage and devastation, and went to reinforce their good friends, the sign demolishers. . . .

There was no longer a way to bear the horror of the scenes taking place in the city. Doors were broken in, stores were pillaged, and the few people left on the street were accosted. . . .

Tired of so many abominations, I decided to leave my house and go (at the risk of being sabered or detained) seek shelter in a calmer neighborhood. . . . I found refuge in a public building, the Flour-Weighing House, where I knew one of the weighers. . . . We covered the lights and cracked the windows to hear what was happening in town. We heard the cries of these lunatics who were becoming more and more numerous; and, among these cries of rage, we distinguished those of the unfortunate victims falling beneath their blows. . . .

On the morning of the 27th, I was ready to learn horrible things about the events of the previous night, but not at all. The gardener was the only man killed, they say. The gunshots we heard were fired in the barracks, as a sign of celebration, they say. And the real damage consists only in several individuals who were wounded, a greater number who

---

[21] A festival to celebrate the liberal constitutional reforms granted by Napoleon after his return from Elba.

were insulted or beaten, many broken-down doors, smashed windows, wrecked signs, and general fright. . . .

June 1815

On Saturday, June 3rd, a large part of the troops in garrison left. They are marching toward the frontiers, where the allies are gathering in large numbers. . . . We are beginning to breathe easier, seeing this horde of Tartars leaving. God spare us from having to see them again! Especially if they are thrown back by the foreigners! . . . From what they have done these last days, one can easily imagine what they would do if they had nothing left to lose! . . .

June 15, 1815: Terror and consternation are still the order of the day. . . . They are working frantically to repair and arm Fort St. Nicolas. . . . Cannons and mortars are being placed there. . . . The rumor is that the intention of the generals who govern us is to force us to hand over all the money they want and conscript all the men they can and bombard us if we refuse or are unable to comply! . . .

This is the point to which we are reduced. . . . While waiting, they are taxing us individually for large sums to pay the cost of repairing the forts, so that we are effectively paying for the switches that will beat us. . . . Toulon was given provisions for a long time and, to do so, they took all the foodstuffs that were here. They made forcible requisitions that ruined many individuals. They took all the carts to transport these supplies to Toulon. There isn't a single person here who wasn't plundered in some way. . . .

Today, June 17th, . . . the more the allies' advance, the more our situation becomes critical and the danger more imminent. God alone knows where this is going. . . . All the pensioned-off officers, who are here in great numbers, have been armed [and] formed into a regiment.

Sunday, June 25th . . . about 1 p.m., there was a great uproar in the city, even though most of the inhabitants had gone to the countryside. But the common people who remained gathered on every corner. The rumor spread that Buonaparte had abdicated a second time, and that the white flag was going to be raised. This seemed to contradict the striking victories that had been announced days earlier, when it was assumed that the emperor's troops had routed the allies. . . .

Nonetheless, the guard posts were reinforced, and part of the sacred battalion was stationed at the Canebière. This is the battalion of pensioned-off officers I spoke about above. They seemed furious and threatened the people with gesture and voice. They were heavily armed, and it was easy to see that they were ready to stake everything they had. . . . In effect, cries of panic were soon heard on the Cours, everyone began to run, and I saw a platoon of seven to eight urban guards face-to-face with these enraged men, who were holding bayonets to their chests. They had wanted to take away an individual, but the urban guard sought to prevent it. However, they managed to explain themselves and no blood was spilled.

But there would have been a lot if Lesueur, commander of the garrison, hadn't come alone on horseback to harangue these madmen. At the end of his harangue, they returned to the fort. Then he harangued the people and told them to be calm, go home, and wait to see what would happen. This order was ignored, and the groups continued to grow.

Commander Lesueur having left, the cavalry began to arrive from the Cours and the Canebière. When they were all there, an individual told them there was a large gathering near Rome Street. They retraced their steps. . . . Soon we heard shots from muskets, carbines, and pistols, and we learned afterward that the cavalrymen had killed an urban guard and wounded several people. The disorder then grew extreme, the people, animated by the good news . . . that Buonaparte had abdicated after having been defeated, gathered together and armed themselves. The cavalry withdrew promptly to its lodgings (not without having given and received several musket shots), all the guard posts were evacuated, and soon the urban guard and people were the masters of the city.

The country folk, fugitives from the free companies, and everyone who had heard what was happening returned in very little time, and from that point, started to take revenge. Several notorious individuals were victims of this reaction, among others the infamous Jeauffroy of Toulon, who was killed by a pistol shot and then dragged into the gutter that crosses the Cours, where his body stayed all night and the night of the 25th to 26th.

But while the populace was busy gawking at it and insulting it, a terrible fusillade was heard from the forts and all attention was drawn there. The troops blockaded in Forts St. Jean and St. Nicolas were shooting at the people on the quays. . . . Several were grievously wounded and some killed. . . .

However, the white flag was flying everywhere, while cockades were donned, but joy did not break out like the first time. Terror and vengeance dominated all spirits. . . . Night was falling, and the enemy was barricaded in our midst, it was necessary to expel him, and, weak and disorganized, the urban guard was of little use. Moreover, the line troops had nothing left to lose. . . .

The night was terrible! . . . Fusillades were heard on all sides. . . .

Finally day broke and calmed our fright a bit. We learned that the troops had left, and that they had been attacked by the free companies who had fired on them and killed several, infantry and cavalry. But it would have been better to have killed none, but disarmed them all, rather than having let them leave for Toulon, where they will hole up. . . .

The morning of the 26th, tensions were extreme, and the people, supported by the free companies, went in mass to all the houses of individuals known for being of Buonaparte's party (already the night before several had been destroyed), but this day many more were wrecked. They threw furniture through windows, broke, smashed, or burned everything they found, leaving nothing but walls. . . . Most of these individuals had fled, but those who were caught met a bad end. . . . One named Bessière, long known as a terrorist, having been discovered, was led onto the Cours and, despite the efforts of the urban guard who wanted to save him by taking him into a café, was taken outside and shot in the middle of the Cours. . . . I saw him led out and killed. . . . Two unfortunate Negresses, the same ones who had followed the bust of Buonaparte when it was being paraded, were assailed by the populace and tried to save themselves by kissing the bust of the king that the market ladies of the Cours had raised up, but they pushed them away, as unworthy of approaching it. They then began to hit them and one was shot. The other was dragged off and thrown into the water; as she was thrashing about, she was also shot. Three other individuals were shot on the Cours.

Much of the day was spent in similar executions. . . . The general alarm was sounded everywhere, and calm seemed to return, but executions continued a bit further off. The countryside was searched and, from time to time, we heard in the distance shots that announced new executions. . . .

July 1815

Saturday, July 8th, around 5 p.m., a courier arrived with an olive branch in his hat, shouting at the top of his lungs "Long Live the King." He told everybody that the allies had entered Paris and that Buonaparte was fleeing. At that news, the people of Marseille went into motion in its accustomed manner, which is to say with lots of noise. An immense crowd went to the Aix Gate to see the couriers arriving from Paris and Lyon. . . .

The day of Sunday, July 9th, which should have been devoted to celebrating the happy news of the allies' entry into Paris, was, to the contrary, a day of fear and sadness for the city of Marseille. . . . At 4 a.m., drumbeats summoned the urban guard, and everybody believed that it was to attend religious ceremonies of thanksgiving. . . . But not at all, it was to assemble all the grenadiers and chasseurs of the urban guard and dispatch them to [the nearby village of] Gardanne, where Brune's horsemen were causing damage. . . . Some said that Brune himself was marching against us with his remaining troops to sack Marseille. . . .

On July 13, 1815, English and Sicilian troops disembarked. . . . They are said to number 4,000, infantry and cavalry. The English wear red, the Sicilians blue: The latter have ancient-style helmets, and the officers resemble theatrical heroes. The horses that were landed are English and very fine and, in general, these troops are handsomely turned out. . . . But despite the urgent need that we had for them in the present circumstance, it is still painful to see foreigners come do for us what we should have done ourselves, that is, to reestablish order and maintain the Bourbons. We are like a great family that, unable to get along, has recourse to lawyers to arrange their affairs. In the end, the lawyers get everything and the legitimate heirs nothing. I am very afraid that that will be our story: We will owe it all to the illustrious Buonaparte and to the scoundrels who betrayed and sold us to support him. . . .

On July 14th, many more English and Sicilian troops landed. . . . Some have been placed in barracks and others billeted on the bourgeois. . . . The market ladies and fishwives held different promenades, carrying the king's bust in triumph, surrounded by many white flags with superb embroidery, gilding, and magnificent accessories. These women were well-dressed in their style; it's a pity that they did not have the idea of dressing all in white. They were preceded by detachments of the urban guard and followed by drummers playing the air *Long Live Henri IV*. The English will not doubt our royalism, thanks to these significant marks and the thousand repeated cries of "Long Live the King" heard on all sides at the passage of the royal bust. The musicians of one of the English regiments, which had halted last night on the quay, also played the air *Long Live Henri IV*, which was greatly applauded.

The 15th, still more English disembarked. It is raining Englishmen. Their current number is estimated to be 15,000 men. . . . It's too much. . . .

September 1815

September 1, 1815, a strong detachment of Austrians entered Marseille, something that we should have been spared, given our good conduct and devotion to the king. To make matters worse, they were billeted on the bourgeois, which was very impolitic given that we are worn out by the sacrifices we ceaselessly make, given that we have been lodging the

English and Italians since their arrival, and given that we would have preferred to have them (given their gentle manners and cleanliness) rather than the vile Austrians, who are dirty as can be and as brutal as Germans. But not at all, the English were lodged in barracks and we were given the newcomers. . . .

These gentlemen arrived as if entering enemy country, acting like masters, demanding whatever they pleased, and threatening if it was not handed over. There were several fights between them and the bourgeois, but when they saw that we were standing up against them . . . they calmed down. But we still had to feed them and give them drink, something fairly difficult, the price of wine having risen daily thanks to their efforts, and it might soon run out altogether because not only are 1,200,000 extra mouths drinking to excess in France, but also because they eat all the grapes and destroy the vines. . . .

The St. Lazare fair was very sad this year, and the city too. Today, September 6th, the Austrians were given 30,000 [francs] as a forced loan, which doesn't put the inhabitants in a good mood. The order was also given to review the urban guard next Sunday with full pomp, cannons, mortars, mounted officers, etc. All this to make an impression on our allies. . . . But this was of little use; the strongest is always right, and we are no longer the strongest. . . .

Friday the 15th, last day of the St. Lazare fair, a troop of French cavalry, about 100 men, arrived. They are lancers, and they cried "Long Live the King," as did the people. But this cry has grown muted since we have felt what it is like to be at the mercy of foreigners and above all when we see that everyone who risked himself for the king has been forgotten and those who betrayed him are rewarded again. This proves that it is not the king who commands and that he is still surrounded by the same men. . . .

Monday night, September 25th, there was a big scuffle in the Comédie neighborhood. A Sicilian soldier was killed and another grievously wounded, but the details vary according to the opinion of whoever is talking. It seems, however that individuals in the free corps attacked the Italians from behind, but out of a particular motivation caused by jealousy over the women of that neighborhood. What is sure is that the leaders were very angry and wanted to have a partisan brawl because they were running in the streets near the Comédie, naked saber in hand and beating up whomever they met. . . . It is a spark that could ignite a large fire. . . . The fear was great, everyone shut themselves up at home, and the night was very stormy, the whole troop was placed on duty; but everything calmed down at last, and the next day it had dissipated.

This is not the only catastrophe caused by jealousy between the bourgeois and the allies. In the upper class, that is to say, between officers and bourgeois, there have been several duels caused by the infidelity or imprudence of the feminine sex, strongly stimulated by the presence of so many young soldiers hungry for women (even though their own women were brought along as a precaution), but since there are not enough to go around, those who are lacking compensate themselves with the local ladies, and this causes much quarreling in families. . . .

October 1815

Saturday, October 7, 1815, the Austrians who were at Marseille left about noon with their excellent musicians, but it is said they are going to nearby towns like Aubagne, Aix, Roquevaire, etc. That's not exactly leaving for good. . . . That same night, Sicilians arrived, so that the lodgings were not empty for long. We didn't even have time to wash the sheets.

Monday, October 9th, tickets were distributed throughout the city for the payment of diverse sums relative to the millions that must be paid to the allies.[22] The smallest tax is 110 francs, and there are some at 800, and always on the property owners, only on them. One way or another, it is always the bourgeois who pay, they are almost ruined. . . . The newly wealthy who have grown fat on our remains pay nothing since they have had the presence of mind to keep their fortune in their wallet. Masséna, Thibaudeau, and so many others keep their treasures, and we pay for them after having been their victims. . . . If that is clemency, it is very misplaced, and if it continues, I think I will stop being a royalist. That is not what we were promised; our misery was supposed to be lessened, but it gets worse each day. . . . They should lower taxes, but they double them each day. The costs of war should be paid by those who brought back the usurper, but it is those who defended the king who are oppressed. . . .

December 1815

According to the peace treaty signed by the king and the allied powers, a treaty contrary to the fine promises they made to the king and the nation, the English, Sicilians, Piedmontese, and other foreign troops who have been at Marseille for several months finally left on December 4, 1815. That is to say that on that day they all boarded transport

---

[22] France had to pay the allies about 1 billion francs in war reparations. This sum was raised through extraordinary taxes and paid off in three years. Upon payment of the indemnity, in 1818, the allied occupying troops left France.

ships to go, they say, to Genoa or Malta. This departure, which did not displease the generality of the inhabitants, given the great expense those people required, made many women of Marseille shed great tears. A crowd of them went onto the quays to say their last goodbyes to their gallant men, but the populace booed them. . . . It is said that there was a household where the mother, two daughters, and a servant were all made pregnant by these messieurs. . . . It is a great honor for my fatherland! Finally, they are gone, leaving behind bastards against whom they will go to war some day. We cannot hope for a solid peace with the English, after the way they conducted themselves with us. Individually, we have nothing to complain about, but nationally, they treat us harshly and that is not what they promised.

A Chronology of the Revolutionary and Napoleonic Wars (1792–1816)

1792 *April 20*   France declares war on Austria; start of revolutionary wars.

1793 *August 23*   France initiates levy-in-mass.

**1796–
1797** *April 1796–April 1797*   First Italian campaign; General Bonaparte achieves fame.

1797 *October 17*   Austria signs Treaty of Campoformio.

**1798–
1799** *May 1798–August 1799*   Egyptian campaign.

1798 *September 5*   France introduces conscription.

1799 *November 9–10*   Napoleon takes power in the coup d'état of 18 Brumaire.

1800 *May–July*   Second Italian campaign and French victory at Battle of Marengo.

1801 *February 9*   Austria signs Treaty of Lunéville.

**1801–
1803** *December 1801–November 1803*   Haitian expedition.

1802 *March 27*   Britain signs Treaty of Amiens.

1803 *May*   Collapse of Peace of Amiens.

1804 *May 18*   Napoleon proclaimed emperor.

1805 *July–August*   Coalition forms between Britain, Russia, and Austria.

October   French victory at Battle of Ulm (20) and British victory at Battle of Trafalgar (21).

December   French victory at Battle of Austerlitz (2) and Austrian surrender (25).

1806 *October 14*   French victories at Battles of Jena and Auerstadt.

November   French occupy Berlin.

November 21   Berlin Decree establishes Continental Blockade.

1807   *February 8*   French-Russian stalemate at Battle of Eylau.

June 14   French victory at Battle of Friedland.

July 7 and 9   Russia and Prussia sign Treaties of Tilsit.

October   French troops enter Portugal and Spain.

November–December   Milan Decrees issued to reinforce Continental Blockade.

1809   *April–October*   War against Austria.

May 21–22   Austrian victory at Battle of Aspern-Essling.

July 5–6   French victory at Battle of Wagram.

July–December   British landing at Walchern.

October 14   Austria surrenders.

1810   *April 2*   Wedding of Napoleon and Marie-Louise of Austria.

July   Napoleon annexes Holland.

December   Napoleon annexes parts of northern Germany.

1812   *June 4*   U.S. declares war on Britain (War of 1812).

1812–
1813   *June 1812–March 1813*   Russian campaign.

1812   *September 7*   French victory at Battle of Borodino.

September 14   French occupy Moscow.

October 18   French begin retreat from Russia.

1813   *March*   Prussia declares war on France.

March 17   Prussia activates Landsturm and Landwehr.

April–June   German campaign.

August 12   Austria declares war on France.

October   French expelled from Spain, pursued by British.

October 16–19   Allied victory at Battle of Leipzig.

December   Allies cross the Rhine; begin invasion of France.

1814   *March 31*   Allies occupy Paris.

April 6   Napoleon abdicates; Bourbons restored (1st Restoration).

1814–
1815   *April 1814–February 1815*   Napoleon in exile on Elba.

September 1814–June 1815   Congress of Vienna.

1815   *March 1*   Napoleon returns to France.

March–June   The Hundred Days.

June 18   Battle of Waterloo.

June 22   Napoleon abdicates.

July 26   Napoleon sets sail for St. Helena, where he dies in 1821.

1815–
1816   White Terror against Bonapartists and Revolutionaries.

Questions for Consideration

1. To what extent and in what ways can the Napoleonic Wars be considered total wars?
2. How did civilians become soldiers? How did soldiers become civilians? How complete were these transformations?
3. How did soldiers and civilians perceive and deal with unfamiliar people, places, and experiences during the Napoleonic Wars?
4. Compare and contrast soldiers' and civilians' experience of billeting, requisitioning, and pillaging.
5. To what extent did ideology, nationalism, and religion motivate soldiers and civilians? What other factors influenced their thoughts and deeds?
6. What role did gender play in shaping the experience of soldiers and civilians during the Napoleonic Wars?
7. How did wartime experiences affect relations between men and women?
8. Compare and contrast the styles of the different kinds of documents (memoirs, diaries, letters, reports). How do differences in literary format influence the way the authors relate their wartime experiences?
9. What effect did war have on civilian life?
10. What was the environmental impact of the Napoleonic Wars?
11. What problems for soldiers, civilians, and governments were raised by the transition from war to peace?

Selected Bibliography

GENERAL OVERVIEW

Blanning, T. C. W. *The French Revolutionary Wars, 1787–1802*. London: Arnold, 1996.

Broers, Michael. *Europe under Napoleon, 1799–1815*. London: Arnold, 1996.

Chandler, David. *Dictionary of the Napoleonic Wars*. New York: Macmillan, 1979.

Connelly, Owen. *Blundering to Glory: Napoleon's Military Campaigns*. Wilmington, Del.: Scholarly Resources, 1999.

Esdaile, Charles. *The Wars of Napoleon*. London: Longman, 1995.

Woolf, Stuart. *Napoleon's Integration of Europe*. London: Routledge, 1991.

TACTICS AND STRATEGY

Muir, Rory. *Tactics and the Experience of Battle in the Age of Napoleon*. New Haven, Conn.: Yale University Press, 1998.

Rothenberg, Gunther. *The Art of Warfare in the Age of Napoleon*. Bloomington: Indiana University Press, 1978.

TOTAL WAR

Bell, David A. *The First Total War: Napoleon's Europe and the Birth of Warfare as We Know It*. Boston: Houghton Mifflin, 2007.

Forrest, Alan, Karen Hagemann, and Jane Rendall, eds. *Soldiers, Citizens, and Civilians: Experiences and Perceptions of the Revolutionary and Napoleonic Wars, 1790–1820*. London: Palgrave-Macmillan, 2008.

Stoker, Donald, Frederick C. Schneid, and Harold D. Blanton, eds. *Conscription in the Napoleonic Era: A Revolution in Military Affairs?* London: Routledge, 2009.

Van Creveld, Martin. *Supplying War: Logistics from Wallenstein to Patton*. Cambridge, U.K.: Cambridge University Press, 1977.

WOMEN AND GENDER

Cardoza, Thomas. *Intrepid Women: Cantinières and Vivandières of the French Army*. Bloomington: University of Indiana Press, 2010.

Lynn, John A. *Women, Armies, and Warfare in Early Modern Europe.* Cambridge, U.K.: Cambridge University Press, 2008.

AUSTRIA

Rothenberg, Gunther. *Napoleon's Great Adversaries: The Archduke Charles and the Austrian Army, 1792–1814.* Bloomington: Indiana University Press, 1982.

BRITAIN

Buckley, Roger Norman. *The British Army in the West Indies: Society and the Military in the Revolutionary Age.* Gainesville: University Press of Florida, 1998.

Cookson, J. E. *The British Armed Nation, 1793–1815.* Oxford: Clarendon Press, 1997.

Emsley, Clive. *British Society and the French Wars, 1793–1815.* London: Macmillan, 1979.

Gee, Austin. *The British Volunteer Movement, 1794–1814.* Oxford: Clarendon Press, 2003.

Houlding, J. A. *Fit for Service: The Training of the British Army, 1715–1795.* Oxford: Clarendon Press, 1981.

Semmel, Stuart. *Napoleon and the British.* New Haven, Conn.: Yale University Press, 2004.

FRANCE

Blaufarb, Rafe. *The French Army, 1750–1820: Careers, Talents, Merit.* Manchester: Manchester University Press, 2002.

Elting, John R. *Swords around a Throne: Napoleon's Grande Armée.* New York: Da Capo Press, 1987.

Forrest, Alan. *Conscripts and Deserters: The Army and French Society during the Revolution and Empire.* Oxford: Oxford University Press, 1989.

———. *Napoleon's Men: The Soldiers of the Revolution and Empire.* London: Hambledon and London, 2002.

Hopkin, David M. *Soldier and Peasant in French Popular Culture, 1766–1870.* Woodbridge, U.K.: Royal Historical Society/Boydell Press, 2003.

Lynn, John A. *The Bayonets of the Republic: Motivation and Tactics of the Army of Revolutionary France, 1791–94.* Urbana: University of Illinois Press, 1984.

Scott, Samuel F. *The Response of the Royal Army to the French Revolution.* Oxford: Clarendon Press, 1978.

Woloch, Isser. *The French Veteran from the Revolution to the Restoration.* Chapel Hill: University of North Carolina Press, 1979.

ITALY

Schneid, Frederick C. *Soldiers of Napoleon's Kingdom of Italy: Army, State, and Society, 1800–1815*. Boulder, Colo.: Westview, 1995.

PRUSSIA

Duffy, Christopher. *The Army of Frederick the Great*. Newton Abbot, U.K.: David and Charles, 1974.
Paret, Peter. *Yorck and the Era of Prussian Reform*. Princeton, N.J.: Princeton University Press, 1966.
Simon, Walter M. *The Failure of the Prussian Reform Movement, 1807–1819*. Ithaca, N.Y.: Cornell University Press, 1955.

RUSSIA

Hartley, Janet M. *Russia, 1762–1825: Military Power, the State, and the People*. Westport, Conn.: Praeger, 2008.
Keep, John L. H. *Soldiers of the Tsar: Army and Society in Russia, 1462–1874*. Oxford: Clarendon Press, 1985.
Lieven, Dominic. *Russia against Napoleon: The True Story of the Campaign of War and Peace*. New York: Viking, 2010.

SPAIN

Esdaile, Charles. *Fighting Napoleon: Guerrillas, Bandits, and Adventurers in Spain, 1808–1814*. New Haven, Conn.: Yale University Press, 2004.
Tone, John L. *The Fatal Knot: The Guerrilla War in Navarre and the Defeat of Napoleon in Spain*. Chapel Hill: University of North Carolina Press, 1994.

Index